Stacks

...pimpin' for life

OG STACK$

Stacks ...pimpin' for life Copyright © 2015 by OG STACK$.

All rights reserved. Printed in the United States of America. No part of this book may be used or reproduced in any manner whatsoever without written permission except in the case of brief quotations embodied in critical articles or reviews.

This book is a work of partial-fiction. However, names, characters, businesses, organizations, places, events and incidents either are the product of the author's imagination or are used fictitiously. Any resemblance to actual persons, living or dead, events, or locales is entirely coincidental.

For information contact:

ghettoinkpublications@gmail.com
info@uptownmediaventures.com

Book and Cover design by Team Uptown and graphic designer Justin Cramer.

ISBN: 978-1-68121-027-8

First Edition: March, 2015

10 9 8 7 6 5 4 3 2 1

This book is dedicated to my Cliffview Hilltop Family, my 10th ward OGs, to Collinwood High, to my Team L.A.U, and my new family members of Uptown Media Joint Ventures; and to all those that had faith in my writings as well as to all my Haters who said I couldn't do it.

I would like to thank my mother, sister Fadiah, for the Love she gave me when the streets showed no love and I would like say rest in the highest heaven to my Father Abdus-Shakur. I would like say "big ups" to my one and only brother Muntasir, to my two daughters Yasmine and Kiara, to my two sons Khayree and Wali (William), my daughters' mother Kimberly Ali, two sisters Asma and Zhulaika, and my brother from another mother Rico (Chill). Also, I would like to send shout outs to Goodgame (Free My Bleed), all my family and friends, to all those on lock down in the Fed's Leavenworth (B - Upper), Mendez, Marquis, Cuzzo, my New York family, my Detroit family Jammat, and last but not least Carrie.

I would like to thank my typist Samantha Strine for putting the finishing touches on my book, my graphic designer Justin Cramer, and a special thanks to K Kelly McElroy. Let's get this money! And I would like to thank anybody else I forgot.

I told y'all I was going to do it!

Chapters	Page
The Pimp's Preamble	
Prologue	
Chapter 1 **Tequila**	13
Chapter 2 **Three Weeks Later**	17
Chapter 3 **The Probation Office**	21
Chapter 4 **Away in Detroit**	29
Chapter 5 **The Russian**	37
Chapter 6 **The P.O. Set-Up**	57
Chapter 7 **Vanity Wash**	71
Chapter 8 **Winter and Garvin**	87
Chapter 9 **Stacks, Back in Ohio!**	107
Chapter 10 **Pimp Choosin'**	111
Chapter 11 **Black Murda**	121
Chapter 12 **"Sin"**	129
Chapter 13 **Off Paper!**	137
About the Author	151

Page intentionally left blank

The Pimp's Preamble

Foolish pimps waste their time and energy on frivolous hoes that keep their pockets empty with weak ass thoughts. Then they complain about the way that they are living their lives - a life which they created in the first place. A "gorilla" pimp is a "weak" ass pimp that is stubborn and refuses to learn the real pimpin' game. They control by force. Real pimpin' is mind over matter for strength is the firm basis on which pimpin' is built upon.

No real pimp can be confronted with the difficulties of a confused hoe; that which he has not the power to meet head on and overcome. There are lessons to be learned by every hoe in order to become a successful hoe. The first lesson is that she must discipline herself to control her speech and speak only when spoken to unless she is speaking about money. Then she must let it be born in the mind that laziness is a disease that can only be cured by clearly having an understanding that procrastination leads to laziness. A hoe must keep a firm, fixed determined mind to do whatever it takes to make and keep her pimp happy.

The first step to doing this is to have dignity about herself. Be proud to be a hoe and be the best hoe that she can be. Realize that being a hoe is not a bad thing to be. Pleasing a man outside of her pimp is the worst thing to do when it comes to doing it for free. Every hoe needs to know that the best things in life do not come free and that a dishonest hoe is a trifling hoe, which is a nasty hoe, that won't last long in the hoe game. As for every pimp that lives life off of his dick and emotions by thinking with the head in between his legs instead of the head on his shoulders – he will eventually become a tender dick emotional non pimping ass "simp." So to all the real pimps keep a thick dick and stay in motion with an EMONTIONLESS HEART.

PIMP OR DIE!

Prologue

Stacks was his name and pimpin' became his game. He was an OG in the game of life who was born in Brooklyn, New York, and grew up Cleveland, Ohio, and lived all over the United States. Throughout his years of being married to the streets, he came to mastering whatever game it was that consisted of him being able to get money - except for the pimpin' and breaking a hoe game. After being incarcerated with the feds Stacks picked up the game from an old-skool pimp by the name of Poppa-Locka who was serving a life sentence for pimpin' and pandering, also known as "white slavery." Stacks switched lanes and started breaking bitches on the internet while pimpin' them from his cell.

His cuzzin Precious was a strip club owner who turned Stacks on to some of the girls working at her strip club for Stacks to pimp out to his fellow convicts. Breaking a bitch and pimpin' a hoe came all the way natural for Stacks. Way before he knew how to define the words bitch, hoe, or pimp, at an early age, Stacks had a young bitch paying him in fifth grade, who carried the name "Redd." She would bring Stacks rings, watches, and money that belonged to her father. She would also give Stacks her lunch money, just to be around him that way she could be able to breath the same air as him as if he was breathing a different type of air then she was. She liked Stacks so much that she would always try to indulge in sexual acts with him. One day Stacks talked Redd into sucking his best friend's dick by the name of KayShawn, who Stacks called "K." Redd agreed to doing this but before she gave K some head Stacks put a charging on K for everything to take place. So when you think about it Stacks was truly destined to be the certified pimp that he became throughout his five years of being incarcerated.

To sum it all up, pimpin' was in his blood the whole time. It just took him being locked up with no-one to rely on except his circle of women that he knocked off by using his mouth piece. What made him fall in love with the game was a bitch by the name of Tequila Ramirez. She was the warden of the federal prison he was serving his time in. She was so fine that she was intoxicating to the eyes and could leave any man bewildered. She had a sexy exotic five feet three inch one hundred and twenty five pound frame. Tequila's eyes were money green. She had a strong resemblance to the Latin singer Selena Quintanilla - God bless the dead.

From the second she graced his eyes with her presence. The only thoughts that entered his mind was how she could help him to generate a major amount of cash flow. That's when he vowed to himself to have her under his control. No doubt, 90 days later, he had total mind control over her. Stacks had devised a plan that involved him operating a prostitution ring. Right up under the Fed's radar for illegal activities, the prostitution ring was disguised as a program for the elite convict. The program provided an extreme safe environment without all the stabbings, killings, and extortion that accrued in the penitentiary, behind the walls of destructions. There were a few small but major requirements that were to be met before being placed into the special housing unit which was D-block. First and foremost you could not have a 5k1, Rule 35 or anything to do with assisting the government in any way in your file - not even on your state police records. So there was an extensive thorough back ground check. Basically no fucking rats, child molesters, or dick sucking faggots were allowed into the program. Especially them faggot mufuckas who thought it was cool to let another man to suck on their dicks.

Then you had to be serving a minimum of 25 years. Plus you had to be able to pay your monthly bill for bed space at $500. That's what made the Feds fall blindly for the program. They were so thirsty that they didn't realize that Stacks was using the warden to build his multimillion dollar empire. You see for $3,000 a person could secure himself a certified hoe who would stay from Friday to Sunday.

Stacks also had his own web site that was ran by Moet, Tequila's identical twin sister. The name of the site was called meetyouafriend.com. He put himself on the site and met a rich white realtor by the name of Jenifer who helped him set up an overseas bank account in the Bahamas. By the time Stacks left prison he had a little over $300,000 in his account, a stable full of hoes, a website, and more game than Parker Brothers.

After he was released back into society, during the time when America was at its lowest, he was left with the only thing to do: Pimp or Die!!!

Chapter 1

Tequila

"Look Tequila I am on to bigger and better things either you with me or not!"

"Stacks you know I'm with you, it's just I don't understand why we have to shut the program down."

"Look 'T' we are not shutting the program down, we are spreading our wings. That's why I asked your sister Moet to step in so we can still get the program money and she can keep the money from the union as the warden," said Stacks.

"With you and her being identical, won't nobody know the difference. And big pimpin' Poppa-Locka; he gone hold shit down for me. You see the way that I see it, is me giving your sister 25 percent, Poppa-Locka 25, and then that leaves me with 50 percent."

"Ok, where do I come in the equation at?" asked Tequila.

"As my bottom bitch, my prize possession, there to handle my empire full of hoes. You understand me. I had Jenifer purchase some acres of land on the outskirts of Las Vegas. That way we can build the "Doll House," not too far from that white boy who owns the Bunny Ranch. Which brings me to letting you know that I'm bringing your girlfriend Tina as the in-house nurse on the property," said Stacks.

"That's not why you bringing that bitch! You bringing her because she suck your dick almost as good as I do!" said Tequila.

"Yeah well for whatever reason I'm bringing the bitch. The hoe coming whether she sucking my dick or licking your pussy. The bitch gone play her position and make sure all my hoes are disease free, as well as physically fit. I had the bitch get her personal fitness training license complements of my pockets so to be technical, I own that bitch - just like I own your ass."

"Stacks just promise me one thing," said Tequila.

"What's that?"

"That you keep your feelings in your heart. I mean I don't have a problem with sharing money and some dick, but when it comes to your heart let that belong to me," said Tequila.

"I told you about that emotional shit. You know I keep it emotionless and in motion at all times – pimpin' at an all-time high. Just be happy and proud to be my bottom bitch. I need you to eat, sleep, and shit my pimpin. Pimpin' is what I do; not who I am although. I am a person intellectually making paper a muthafucking P to the I.M.P and don't you ever forget that."

"Stacks my whole life is about keeping you happy and I know that the only way to keep you happy is to give you the only thing that make you happy; and that's money."

"No Tequila it's not the money it's what the money does for me and that's making a way for me to make more money. Your job is to be the team captain when it comes to the other females. Oh yeah did you make that call to my cuzzin Precious and if so what did she say about being at the front gate to pick me up?"

"She said some-thing about your homeboy K was coming with her," said Tequila.

"Dam that's my nigga. K kept it real the whole time I was in and my Big Homey Moe-Bling from Detroit, those two are the realest muthafuckers I ever met!"

K and the big homey Moe-Bling were Stack's friends since he had bitches in the sand box building him sand castles. Stacks slipped into a deep train of thought thinking back on the time that him and K rain a train on Ms. Maritza.

Ms. Maritza, was their Spanish teacher from Collinwood High School. Stacks was always a verbal gymnast when it came to flipping his tongue and putting the right words where they were supposed to be. He had talked Ms. Maritza into giving him, along with K, private tutoring lessons after school. She had felt so comfortable with the both of them she started holding the lesson at her house in South Euclid on Green Road, right up the street from Cliffview.

After a couple of weeks of Stacks talking shit and swallowing spit. Stacks had Ms. Maritza's fine ass down on all fours deep throating K's dick while he was pounding her in from the back.

Tequila's voice brought Stacks back to the present moment.

"What were you thinking about that got you grinning from ear to ear," said Tequila.

"I was just thinking about how silly K is," said Stacks.

"Well Stacks it's almost count time you better get back to the block."

"Alright Tequila I'll see you tomorrow."

"Alright Stacks daddy. I Love you."

Chapter 2

Three Weeks Later

"**W**ell big pimpin' Stacks; today is your day to shine. Remember purse first, ass last, set the trend, and know that where pimpin begins, friendship end. Pimp like you hoeless and stay ten hoes down for your crown.

"I see you been reading the *Forty-Eight Laws to the Game* by Pimpin' Ken. Well you know what they say young pimp - what's that skool? Knowledge is power and with power you will be able to be the puppet master."

"Alright O.G, I shall keep it pimpin' at all times. It's been real and I appreciate the game. As soon as I get shit started I'll get at you but until then I need you to hold the program down. I even told that hoe Moet to move you over to D-block in the big cell. Alright Big-Pimpin I'm outta here!" said Stacks. They dapped up and on the way out Poppa-Locka said, "Pimp on, Pimpin, pimp on!!"

As soon as Stacks finished dressing out in his new expensive clothes and slipping into a pair of "Finnix" gators laced with ostrich in them, Stacks felt like a born again man. Upon exiting the front gate he noticed two black stretch hummers sitting on 30 inch chrome wheels.

Precious had brought fresh meat - three of the sexist bitches to swing on a pole with her from her strip club, to welcome Stacks home. Precious and K exited one hummer while the bitches exited from the other hummer.

"Yo what up Stacks, you big ass an ox," said K.

"What's good with you K," Stacks said giving him some dap. Then Stacks grabbed Precious and gave her a big hug saying "What up lil-Bleed?"

"Dam Stacks you is on swole! What the fuck you been doing your whole five years; living in the weight room?" said Precious.

"Hell naw, ain't no weights in that raggedy muthafucka, this come from pushups sit ups pull ups, and dips while eating the right foods."

"Yeah Tequila said you were a vegetarian and on the healthy heart diet while you were in."

"I was a vegetarian because they didn't know how to cook in that bitch." Stacks turned to the hoes and looked them up and down. All three were dime pieces and they all looked like they were just getting out of prison their selves, with their bodies all toned up.

"Stacks these three are my gifts to you. This is Summer, Carmela, and Winter," said Precious.

The girls waved and said "hi" then the one with the Carmel skin tone named Carmela stepped forward and extended her hand and said, "I have heard so much about you from the other girls that worked for you on the inside and I've been waiting on this day for quite some time now. Me and my girls brought you a welcome home present."

Then shorty who had on a belly shirt with her navel pierced and a pair of tight fitting hip hugging jeans reached inside of the hummer. Stacks could see a tattoo tramp stamp that read: Summer. She turned around with a gold platter full of rolled up bank rolls and that's when Winter, a thick ass chick resembling Mariah Carrie, took the tray from Summer and said, "We don't know what your choosing fee is but if this don't cover it then just look at it is as a down payment from the three of us."

"Now that's what I call pimpin,'" said K with a big ass smile on his face.

"I don't know what you smiling for you better get your ass back in the truck before I start a scene out in this bitch," replied Precious.

"I see the both of you two still playing house," said Stacks.

"So where are we headed?" asked the limo driver.

"To Ohio. That's where I am supposed to report within 72 hours to my probation officer; on the way back to the land of heartless felons 'O.H 10,'" as them Cleveland players called it.

Stacks was entertained by three wet pussies and some of the best head he ever had. Instantly he knew which one who would be his starting player on his team which would also be who he would play against Tequila to keep her on her toes, so that she can know that if she ever fell short of following his instructions that she would look better leaving then she did coming.

That woman was none other than Summer. She had a hot sexy looking ass and a nice pair of firm breasts that set straight up at attention. Her nipples were hard and you could see her areolas through her all white Prada shirt. She had a pair of lips so full with her lip gloss popping you would have thought they were strictly made to stay wrapped around a dick, not to mention she was the one who initially pulled the banks rolls out on a 24 carat solid gold platter which was now Stack's golden rule - put all money on the golden platter.

Chapter 3

The Probation Office

"My rules are simple to follow and for the next year if you follow them you will be released off of probation. No dirty drug tests or new charges are acceptable at all," said Mr. Malone.

Mr. Malone was an older fat white guy who looked like he was the biggest trick in the world.

"You won't have to worry about me violating Mr. Malone, in no fashion or form. My goals consist of me finding a job and paying my fines while working towards getting off probation. Speaking of fines, here is something towards my fine." Stacks handed Mr. Malone a fresh C-note. He could have just paid the whole fine but he was playing the role of not having any money because he didn't want to make it obvious that he had money long as train smoke.

"I noticed that you also completed a few drug classes while you were in. I hope that your past addiction to P.C.P won't be a problem for you."

"No. It won't be a problem with me relapsing at all with any drugs or alcohol. I am going to find me a home group and work in the program," said Stacks.

"Ok then our time is up and you have a copy of all the rules and regulations. Your color is green so make sure you call in every day before 12:00 noon to see if it's your day to give a specimen of urine. Good luck and have a nice day."

"You too Mr. Malone, bye."

"Well, what did your probation officer say to you," asked K.

"You know the same ole bull-shit about not catching a new charge, staying drug-free, get a job, and don't miss any of my appointments. I squared up in that bitch had him thinking that he had a rehabilitated man who was going to abide by all the rules and requirements. By the way, what did your man say about them paystubs so that I can start turning them in to my P.O.?"

"He said you good, just let him know when you want him to start you on his pay roll."

"Well, tell him to start punching me in starting next week."

"No doubt, I'll get right on that and you got his ends right?"

"Yeah what's the ticket?"

"He wants ten racks for the year and you'll get a pay check every other week for a year which will actually be your ten stacks back. Then he want another ten for the whole process," said K.

"Now where you say his car wash is at?"

"It's on St. Clair off of 55th it's called: One Way Auto Wash & Detail Shop."

"Cool. Cash bleed out with the money and find out if we can offer him some money for the whole joint. Let him know I will let him run the spot but I got some ideas for a car wash and I need that joint.

One thing I do know is that I won't be smoking any wet no-more. The last time I smoked some water I end up calling the police on myself. That's how I caught that fed case in the first place. I never told anybody because I was too embarrassed!" said Stacks.

"What you mean you called the police on yourself?" said K.

"Look, remember that rich white bitch I was fucking named Nicole from Akron?"

"Oh yeah, I remember shorty. She's the one whose father is a race car driver. Didn't she own a hair salon?"

"Yeah no doubt. The bitch was a spoiled fucking brat always getting into shit trying to make her daddy look bad. She did some time before in Marysville down in Southern Ohio for robbing a neighborhood bar. That made it impossible for her to legally buy a gun. So we did a favor for a favor. In return for her making me part owner of the salon, which allowed me the opportunity to clean my dirty money up, I got her a gun. After her house got broken into and she was hospitalized from getting beat up and raped, I used one of my fake I.D's and purchased the bitch a gun from the gun store. I let her hold on to the gun for her own protection.

"Then a week later I got a call when I was chillin' in the pool at my house in Houston. She said somebody broke into the house again."

"Man Stacks what the fuck all that got to do with you smoking wet?" asked K.

"If you shut the fuck up and let me finish I'll tell you what the fuck it got to do with me smoking wet! On one of my trips to Ohio I slid by the salon, got her key to the house, and went there to relax till she got off. While I was kicked back I blazed a Dutch full of that good purple and dunked that bitch in some of that "butt naked." But instead of me getting naked I called the police after getting paranoid after I saw the news.

The news story talked about a guy who had just been released from prison after being wrongfully convicted for a murder he didn't do. He was in prison for 22 years. His gun was found at the murder scene and it took 22 years for them to find out the truth from a guy with a guilty conscious on his death bed, who admitted to the murder, and gave a detailed account. That's when I called Nikki to see if she had reported the gun stolen. She said that she 'only reported the miscellaneous stuff and not the gun.'

"Then two more sticks later they showed the guy again saying that only if he would had made a police report about his gun being stolen he would have never went to prison in the first place. That's when the voice in my head said 'if you don't want that to be you, then you know what you have to do.'

"So I picked up the phone, called 911, and told the dispatcher that I just got back into town and wanted to make a report about a stolen gun that I left at my girl-friend house in the celling. I told her that my girl had already made a report about the house being broken into but she didn't know that my gun was in the house. The dispatcher said she was sending a squad car to me to make a report in person.

"When the squad car pulled up. I opened the door drenched off three sticks to the head and a couple of shots of "Hen." I was so fucked up that before I realized what I did. I was standing there explaining to the police were the gun was. Then a police officer asked me for my name. I told him the name that I brought the gun under. Then the other cop asked me for some I.D. I gave him my real I.D.! He noticed that it was different from the name I just gave his partner and said that the I.D I gave him didn't match the name I just gave his partner. Then the officer asked: 'are you that high that you don't know your own name?'

"I said here is the I.D that goes with the gun. That I.D is who I really am. But I've been living under the other I.D because I have warrants back home in Brooklyn NY for a probation violation. The officer asked 'can you repeat that?' So I did. Then he told me he needed to finish his report down at the police station. Then he asked me did I mind coming with him. I said that I didn't mind just let me grab my truck keys.

"The black cop said 'you can just ride with us that way you can save gas.' He knew I was fucked up. At that time the gas prices were sky high so I thought that I would be really saving on gas. So I said fuck it and rode with them."

"Bleed that's some funny ass shit you need to tell that story to that TV show, the *Dumbest Criminal*. I guarantee you will win a quick ten thousand for that shit!"

"Look you just keep that shit to yourself, real talk, Bleed."

"Yeah no doubt I got you Bleed I won't put that shit out there to nobody," said K.

"The craziest part about it …"

"Hold on man you mean to tell me that it's more to that shit?!"

OG Stack$

"Yeah! after I was in the county for a few days this racist ass sons anarchy white boy was on the phone next to me begging and pleading his love to his bitch. He was talking about the only reason he beat her up was because when they was fucking he heard her say she love him but she said another man's name. So then he asked her 'who the fucks is Stacks?' That's what caught my attention.

"So when he got off the phone I asked him what he was in there for. He said for assaulting his girl that he been with for ten years who was cheating on him with some guy named Stacks. So I asked him was his girl named Nicole? He said yeah. That's when I flipped out on his ass. Not because of the bitch playing me but because I felt like a sucka for love ass nigga that let his emotions for a bitch get him caught up, plus he was the one that stole my gun. That's why bro, a bitch can't get nothing outta me but some hard dick and some bubble gum. I'm fresh out of gum so all she can get is the dick, which gone cost her ass top dollars!"

"Dam Stacks you one crazy muthafucka for that one but I feel you on that Big Hommie! I still say you one lucky, unlucky muthafucka. All the dope you sold then, jewelry stores you robbed, and it took a muthafucking wet tick to get you caught up. That's except for that time in high school when you shot ole boy for fucking your ends ups."

"Well that's the past and now I home stronger than when I left with a fleet full of hoes all selling pussy for me. Oh yeah, one last thing I forgot to mention. I need you to check with a few of your business colleagues and get any and all information you can on Donald Malone. That's my P.O. and I need to get some shit on him so I can pull his strings and I need that info as soon as I get back from Detroit - this week."

"Alright I'll get straight on that for you."

Chapter 4

Away in Detroit

"Tequila! Tequila!" called out Precious.

"Hey Precious. How you doing?"

"Oh, I'm good girl. What about you?"

"I'm alright just exhausted from the plane ride. Where's Stacks at?" asked Tequila.

"He had to take care of some business in Detroit. His plane just left about 20 minutes ago," said Precious.

"He didn't tell me he was going to Detroit and for what reason did he go to Detroit?" said Tequila.

"Now that I couldn't tell you but your plane is an hour late and he tried to wait around for you but you know it's always business first with him," said Precious.

"I know, it's just that it's been almost a month since he got out and I haven't had a chance to see him on this side of the wall."

"Trust me the only thing that has changed about him is that he is back to making major moves all over again."

"Oh there my bags go can you grab those while I grab these?"

"You sure brought enough shit with you," said Precious.

"Girl I only brought a few things," said Tequila as she was laughing.

"Anyway Stacks left a few bands and told me to take you shopping for some new shit. He said that warden look isn't gone get it in this line of business," said Precious.

"Did he tell u when he was coming back from Detroit?" asked Tequila.

"He'll be back tomorrow night. We will have a meeting at the club with the girls." They grabbed the luggage and headed straight to Beachwood Mall.

Precious' phone started to ring. She looked at the number on the phone and pressed the send button to answer the call.

"Hello," said K.

"Hey," responded Precious.

"Where you at Precious?"

"I'm at the mall in Beachwood with Tequila, why you ask baby - is everything ok?"

"Yeah I'm good, the reason why I called is because I wanted to know did you want to go out to dinner tonight?" asked K.

"Yes baby you know I do. Where are we going to go eat at?

"I figured that we could go to Maggianos in Beachwood."

"Sounds good to me," said Precious.

"Alright then, I'll pick you up about seven."

"No I'll just meet you there if that is alright with you."

"Cool don't be late. I'll be there at seven."

"I won't be late baby."

"Ok then, later," said K who then hung up the phone before Precious could respond.

Precious was so excited being able to see K that night because she had not seen him since Stacks been out and she wanted to see her man.

"Tequila, we have to make this fast because I'm going to dinner with K tonight and I want to get ready so I can be on time. His fine ass always drive me crazy just thinking about him," said Precious.

"To be truthful I'm through. I already got what I needed and that's me some Victoria Secret so I can look sexy in something when Stacks come home," said Tequila.

"Cool we out then. We can hit New York up next week. Then we can both spend some money," said Precious.

They pulled up to house and went in.

"Tequila, Stacks' room is at the top of the stairs off to the right. Don't worry about the bags just leave them in the car and I'll have one of the girls to grab them for you."

"Girl I wasn't about to grab no bags anyway I'm too tired to be lugging them bags in. I'm headed upstairs to go to sleep."

Precious took a fresh shower, put on her new Prada outfit with her three inch heels and headed out of the house. Then she went to get to the car and noticed the bags were still in the back seat. So she decided to take Stacks' 745 BMW.

They pulled up to the restaurant around the same time. First Precious pulled up and while the valet was grabbing her keys K pulled up. They walked into the spot and K gave the lady at the door the name that the reservations were under, then they were escorted to their table.

Precious had all kind of thoughts running through her head. She was craving his energy.

"So how you been bobee K?" said Precious snapping out of her deep thoughts.

"Every-thing is good, what about you?

"You know shit crazy stupid with Stacks home and he got me running around all over town taking care of the legal part of his illegal business, but besides that I'm good."

"Good evening may I take your order?" the waiter asked.

"What you having Precious?"

"Well, I'll have the Pasta Primavera with Italian turkey sausage and a side of salad."

"And you Sir?"

"I'll have what the lady is having."

They ate talked and laughed about old times. Then after dinner Precious invited him to come back to the house. Once in the house K didn't waste no time. He started kissing her very passionately. She pushed him back and said, "Follow me. Tequila is here somewhere and the girls are here as well. Stacks had them stay in till he get back."

So they went to Precious' room. Once in the room she started kissing all over him. He began unbuttoning her blouse and removing her bra. She reached for his dick that seemed to be bulging through his pants. He put one of her breasts in his mouth. His tongue felt extra wet and soft, she thought to herself.

She started unzipping his pants and pulled out his dick - then she paused and smiled because every time she laid eyes on the thirteen inch python. It made her overly excited to know that in any minute she would be feeling his dick up deep inside her. His dick was fully erect so she dropped to her knees and started licking and sucking the sides like an ice-cream that was melting in her hands moving her tongue in circles around the top. She was mentally preparing herself to deep throat it.

She kept caressing it with her tongue. He was grunting and moaning telling her to suck it. "Baby put it in your mouth," he said. She attempted to take it all down her throat but to no avail. She started gagging as he started pumping her face. This went on for what seemed like forever to her as he kept moaning and shouting "Suck it, keep sucking it baby!"

Her jaws were hurting and she was tired of sucking him but she kept going like a champ until he laid her on the floor and put her legs on his shoulders then started squeezing her left nipple while rubbing her clit with the other hand. His touch was so sensual to her then he stuck his tongue in and out of her wet pussy. Her pussy lips were so fat that it reminded him of a Big Mac and he was trying to devour it.

In one move while sucking on her clit he then started fingering her with his middle finger which made her start shaking as she slipped into a deep trance as he brought her to a climax he kept sucking while she was cumming which made her have a multiple orgasms in the mist of her cumming.

He positioned her and put the head of his dick in her pussy. She started squirming as he inched his way in until he had a nice amount in her - then he started stroking. She was letting out loud moans and grunts as he pushed all thirteen inches into her. She could feel it way up in her stomach. She thought that she was about to pass out from him fucking her so hard. He banged her all around on the floor for hours. Then he turned her around and started fucking her doggy style. She could feel her cervix being ripped apart. It was starting to hurt and K knew this because she was now screaming saying, "K please baby please I can't take it no more please!" Then she felt him swelling up as he was at the point of no return.

He pulled his dick out and shoved it down her throat exploding deep in her neck. She could feel his juices rushing to her stomach. She swallowed his cum as she was sucking and liking on it like a candy cane.

Shortly afterwards they laid there in each other's arms. Precious thought to herself how much she loved it when he just took total control over her body, then she made a mental note to put some ice on her pussy in the morning to bring the swelling down.

Chapter 5

The Russian

"Hello sir, how may I help you today?"

"I need two suites joined together if they are available."

"I have singles, doubles, and the executive suites. Which one will you be taking sir?"

"Give me the two executive suites. Thank you!"

"How many nights will you be staying? One night. Ok, that will be huh, a total of $850 at $425 for each suite. Will that be cash or credit?" said the man at the front desk.

"I'll be paying with my prepaid 'Rush' card."

"Ok, Mr. Stacks is it?"

"Yes, that is what the card says, right?"

"Yes sir. My apologies. I didn't mean to offend you sir. Here are your keys cards. If you happen to lose them it will be a three dollar replacement fee. Have a nice day and enjoy your stay."

Stacks brought Summer, Sin and Mandy with him to Detroit. Sin was an Asian college student here in America on a student visa. She was 4' 8" tall and 132 lbs, thick in all the right places, who loved that she was able to make money doing what she do best - pleasing a man.

Mandy was of Portuguese and German descent who looked like Rosie Perez. Her breasts were perfectly round and she had a gap in between her legs that always displayed how fat her pussy was through any pair of jeans she would wear.

Once everybody reached the suites, Stacks told Summer to meet him down stairs at the hotel bar in thirty minutes. Thirty minutes later Stacks was sipping on some Patron, then Summer came walking in.

"What is it you need to talk to me about?" said Summer.

"Who said I needed to talk about anything?" said Stacks.

"Well, I assumed that by asking me down here without Sin or Mandy, something was on your mind."

"Actually there is something that I need to discuss with you and that is the first time I laid my pimpin' eyes on you... I knew you was a hoe above the rest who was blessed with the potential to be the best hoe that ever could be with the right pimpin' in your corner. See so when you chose up to hoe up, I knew your hoe game would grow up. Put it like this I need that one bitch that's gone sell pussy from sun up to sun down and sell pussy in her sleep for my mutha-fucking crown. Bitch can you do that?"

"Stacks, I'm ready willing and able to do it all! I like it hard and take it deep and if I sold pussy in my sleep for you it won't be cheap. I am a high priced hoe that's like a fireman always ready to go."

"Now you talking bitch, but I need you to get to walking and take the girls to the casino and bring me back some money. We got one night before we get back on the road. Instead of us flying we will be driving back to the city. Tell Mandy and Sin I said to get in where they fit in and get my muthafucking dividends! I need to see at least $10,000 by the time we leave and whatever they don't make, break yo back and get my stacks alright?"

"Ok Stacks. Oh yeah and my platter is on the dresser in my room."

"You know what to do - hoe down baby!"

Ring, Ring, Ring! 'Dam Moe pick up the phone,' Stacks thought to himself. On the third ring Moe picked up the phone.

"Yo what up with it Big Moe?"

"What up doe, is this my nigga Stacks?"

"No doubt bleed," replied Stacks.

"Dam bruh when you get out?"

"O about three to four weeks ago."

"So what state you in my nigga?"

"Right now I'm smashing a pizza at Pizzapapalis."

"Ok so you then slid in on a nigga on the smooth tip. Where you headed after that? To your spot on the east side?" said Moe.

"Naw, I'm staying at the Greek Town Hotel. I need to holla at you Big Moe," said Stacks.

"Ok, when you talking?"

"As soon as possible! What about in an hour, meet me at Hamtramck Sammy's, the cell phone spot. You know the one on Joseph compo," said Stacks.

"Alright Stacks I'll be there in an hour bro."

"Alright bleed!"

"Alright, later!"

As soon as Stacks finished eating, he tipped the waitress, left the restaurant, and hoped in the Cadillac truck that he rented from the airport when he landed. As he was pulling up to Sammy's he noticed how much the neighborhood changed.

"What's up Sammy?" said Stacks.

"Oh shit if it's not money making Stacks himself! What's it been, five years?"

"Yeah Sammy, you know how long it's been. I hope you got that money you owe me because I need it like a trick need a bitch," said Stacks.

"Come on to the back so we can talk," replied Sammy.

When they walked to the back, Sammy went to his safe in the wall behind a picture of him in Jerusalem holding an AR15.

"Well, I have one hundred fifty here. I can go to the bank in the morning and withdraw the rest in the morning if that's all right with you since you just popped up on me out of nowhere Big Money."

"How about you just giving me twenty of them Boost Mobile phones with unlimited internet access paid up for two years and we can call it even on the other fifty because that's small things to a giant a balloon to a blimp, you know, like a bitch to a pimp."

Stacks' phone started ringing. He answered his phone recognizing the number as Big-Moe's phone.

"Hold on Sammy. What up Big-Moe you outside?"

"Yeah, I'm' across the street at Yemen's Chicken ordering me some halal food."

"Alright give me a minute and let me finish up here then I'll be out in a minute. I need you to follow me back to the room."

"Cool bro I'm with that."

"Alright one!"

"Here you go Stacks. Twenty phones and I put you in the computer paid up for the next two years. If by any chance you have any problems, then just give me a call."

"I knew I could count on you Sammy. It's been real, stay up."

"You to Stacks. Anytime, you know I got you."

Stacks and Sammy shook hands and Stacks headed out to load the truck up. Once he was finished loading up the truck he called Big-Moe.

"Big-Moe I'm loaded up and ready to go!"

"Alright I'm coming out right now."

Once outside Stacks gave Moe the run down on why he needed him to follow him so Moe followed Stacks back to the room. Once they were in the room Stacks dumped the cash onto the floor. Big-Moe came in rolling up some of Detroit's finest - none other than some Gannes.

"Big-Moe when you get done rolling up I need you to help me count this money," said Stacks.

"What! You about to count all that money by hand?"

"Hell naw! I'm about to use the machine to count it. All I need you to do is put rubber bands around the money in ten thousand dollar stacks."

"Go ahead stacks I'm with you."

It took a minute to get everything done. When they were finished Stacks blurted out a quote from a Jay-z joint: "men lie, women lie, but numbers don't lie."

Big-Moe took a heavy drag on the blunt and started coughing then said, "Stacks I see you touching paper all over again."

"Yeah, you know me, I gotta stay with that gwaup."

"Well you know you can always come work a legal job with me at my corporate office as my right hand man. I mean you won't be seeing money like this but at least you won't have to worry about going back to prison."

"You know what Moe? Since them white folks scared the shit out of you with that little bit of time you did in the Hamtramck jail, for hitting that punk in the head with that hammer, you like a Johnny b-good type of nigga scared to take a chance."

"It's not that I'm sacred, it's that I'm smarter then you. I took an installation job to owning my own corporate carpet business 'Royalty Carpets.' How that sound nigga?" replied Big-Moe.

"Like a lame ass nine to five. I don't knock you for what you do but I'm into pimpin' hoes now cause ain't no money like hoe money."

"Oh so now you got women who fear you selling their bodies in return to keep you off their backs?" said Moe.

"Nigga, I didn't say gorilla pimpin' I said pimpin'. Do you know what's stronger then fear?" asked Stacks.

"No. What's that?"

"Hope! Hope is stronger than fear. I give a bitch hope that one day she'll have a better life. That's why my bitches stay loyal to me and don't jump ship. If you got a bitch selling pussy for you out of fear it is only so long before she run to another muthafucka who she think that will protect her from you. That's why I give my bitches hope. It's like dangling a rabbit in front of a greyhound dog at a race track. As long as the greyhound sees the rabbit he'll run all day chasing the rabbit with the hope of catching it; but never does. I'm just hiding the gun behind a smile to keep my bitches selling pussy. To keep it simple I motivate a bitch to want to participate in making me rich. Now tell me how that sound nigga," said Stacks.

"To you be your way Stacks and to me be mine. So where these hoes at that you speaking on," asked Big-Moe.

"They down stairs checking paper. What I needed to see you for is to have you install some carpet in this house I'll be buying out in Southfield. I need you to install some of the most expensive carpet that money can buy, from wall to wall, throughout the whole entire house. Here goes twenty stacks to get it done," said Stacks handing over the money to Big-Moe.

"Man this is way too much money for all that."

"Yeah, I know, but this to secure the best dam job to ever be done by you."

"Ok, I'll need the address and the keys."

"Don't worry about that. My realtor bitch gone call you and meet up with you in a couple of days," said Stacks.

"Alright cool," said Big-Moe.

"Ok, I gotta go hit the casino to see what the hoes doing. It's been a few hours since they left so I'll get at you later."

"Stay up Stacks."

"You too, Big-Moe."

Sin came prancing into the room just as Big-Moe was leaving smiling from ear to ear.

"Hi Stacks daddy?"

"What's up Sin, I was just headed down to check out the scene with you and the other girls."

"Stacks that won't be necessary because the other girls are on a date right now. Summer is in room 224 and Mandy left to go over to the M.G.M with this Russian guy," said Sin.

"She shouldn't have did that," said Stacks.

"I came to put this money up," said Sin.

"So how much you got?"

"Well, between Summer and Mandy they got six thousand," said Sin.

"What about you?" said Stacks.

"Well, I came up by myself. Because Summer said that you wanted at least ten thousand before we leave tomorrow and that's supposed to be between the three of us. Well daddy, I made fifteen thousand off of this drunk trick ass white man. I told him that I wasn't fucking or sucking for nothing less than fifteen."

OG Stack$

"So what you want a Scooby snack bitch?"

"No daddy he agreed to it then I told him he had one hour or one nut, which ever one come first. So I pulled out a condom and sucked his dick his until his dick got hard then straddled his drunk ass and 10 seconds later with me riding him he shot his rocket. He paid me in chips from the casino so here is your money."

She opened her Gucci tote bag and poured the chips onto the floor. "Bitch! Do I look like a muthafucking slot machine? And next time don't take any chips because a muthafucka can say you robbed him! So get your Lucy Lu looking ass up and go cash them chips in. After that bring my money back then go find that dumb ass white man with all that paper and spend the night with him for some more of his money. Just because I said I wanted ten thousand don't mean that's where your hoeing stop at."

"I was only thinking," said Sin. Stacks cut her off, "That's your problem trying to use your head instead of being somewhere giving head. Now excuse yourself, because now you got my head doing shit it ain't supposed to be doing and that's hurting. So get the fuck out my face bitch and get back to sucking dicks and turning tricks!"

"Ok daddy. I'm sorry."

"Bitch don't be sorry, be cleaver and realize that I am trying to open your eyes to make the clear view even sharper. You the best bitch I got and I want you to be smooth Sin. You gone be my bottom bitch. Just play the cut like a Band-Aid and follow my lead baby. Now go get yourself together so you can go take care of business."

"Ok Stacks," said Sin.

The rest of the day Stacks spent his time on the black-jack table, drinking on his favorite drink, Patron. Then out of nowhere Summer appeared with a worried facial expression.

"Stacks! Have you seen Mandy?"

"No! I haven't why you ask?"

"Well, it's been six hours ago when she left with this guy headed over to M.G.M."

"Well she probably found her a lame with some deep pockets. Who she working the shit out of, carrying him like mark he is."

"It's just, we got this thing with each other and that is, no matter what, after the fourth hour of leaving for a date we check in with each-other."

"Mandy grown enough to take care of herself what you trying do? Go over there and rain on her parade?" said Stacks.

"No! I just want to make sure that she is ok! Please daddy!"

"Alright go get Sin then meet me out front in ten minutes."

As they pulled up to the M.G.M garage Stacks spotted this tender dick ass nigga by the name of G-Money who he used to get money with a few years back before he went to the Fed's. They worked the shit out of the west side of Detroit. Stacks thought to himself, 'for the life of me, I can't believe how a lame like G-Money knocked Meme's fine ass off only to blow the whole relationship by lying on his dick, telling everybody that he was smashing on her a regular. The nigga even said she had a pussy so fat that it looked like a swollen camels toe when he never even saw what it was shaped like, let alone fucked. All the money they made doing muthafucka taxes that year, now here he go with a 'I will work for money' sign in front of the M.G.M - the same casino where they blew money on many occasions. Dam! Meme really fucked that nigga's head up! I could only imagine what would have happened if she would have put that red snapper on his ass.'

"There go a parking spot daddy," Summer said bringing Stacks back to the present. Stacks pulled in and threw the truck in park. Stacks gave orders to meet back up at the truck in two hours because the sun was coming up and he wanted to get back to the room, especially since all that money was being left unattended. Once inside Stacks walked around looking for Mandy for about an hour, then he tried his wrist on the crap table. He put up ten thousand and rolled a four. He put another ten on ten.

"Four, come on four! I need you," he said as he rolled and the dice landed on ten so he won ten thousand. Then he rolled again and craped out. He looked at his Rolex then started making his way to the truck.

"Alright ladies, any luck in finding Mandy?"

"No we didn't find her," said Sin.

"Well lets go cause I'm ready to kick back," said Stacks.

When they got back to the hotel they all went into Stacks suite. Then he noticed the extra money that was on the platter and he turned to Summer and asked her did she come up to the room before they went to the M.G.M. She said "no" as she was pulling out the money she had made earlier.

Stacks looked over on his bed and noticed a note that was on his pillow he picked it up and start reading it: 'Stacks this is Mandy. I'm ok, I put forty three hundred on the platter. I'll be back later before check out time. I'm with this Russian guy. Love Mandy.'

"See girls, I told you she was alright. Now go lay down and get you some rest. Check out time will be here before you know it. Sin you stay here and get in the shower. I got a special treat for you."

"Ok Stacks," said Summer as she was leaving. Sin went straight to the shower to clean up. When she came out of the shower she stood in front of Stacks who was laying in the bed watching some cable show. She dropped her towel and pulled the bed sheets back. Stacks pulled her towards him then took her right "titty" in his hand then started sucking on her nipple. She started breathing heavy and he started rubbing her pussy that was dripping juices down the left side of her leg.

She moved up close to bring her breast together so he could suck on both nipples. Before she knew it he had three fingers in her pussy making the come here motion maneuvering them deeper in her stomach - unleashing more juices until she was brought to an orgasm. Then she pushed him back on the bed, bent down, and wrapped her mouth around his dick as she started sucking his dick going in circular motions with her tongue. She was moving up and down and across it with her tongue softly blowing on it not using her hands. She tried to deep throat him but couldn't manage to take all of him into her throat. She was making love to his dick with her mouth.

Stacks laid there enjoying her wet warm tight mouth till he couldn't take it anymore. He then pulled her up towards him and lifted her ass up. She mounted him trying to ease down on his dick. Only half of his dick was inside her when, from the thickness, she started to cum all over his dick like Niagara Falls.

She couldn't handle his big ass dick. She felt the top of his dick up by her pelvis - the shit was hurting but in a good way. So that she wouldn't rip her pussy in half she leaned forward and put an arch in her back with her hands on his chest. She slowly rode his dick bouncing up and down at a slow pace but increased her pace which allowed her to take in more of his dick inch by inch until he wrapped his arms up under her legs making them rest on his shoulders.

He stood up cupping her ass in his hands while he pushed his dick all the way up inside her. He was now fucking her standing; deep in her guts - up, back and forth, up and down on his dick. She started shaking saying, "I'm cumming daddy! I'm cumming! Please fuck me harder! Harder pleeeeazz."

So Stacks laid her on the bed and put her in the "hucka buck." As he locked in she couldn't do nothing but scream at the top of her lungs. She was begging him to stop as he went deep and hard hitting her G-spot making her cum over and over with multiple orgasms.

Stacks fucked her all over the room dogging the shit out of her Asian little tight pussy. Never before out of her 24 years of living did she think a dick could hurt as bad as it did, but feel so good at the same time. She was screaming and breathing so loud that Summer, who was in the next room, could hear through the walls as she finger fucked herself to the moans, grunts, and screams of Sin being fucked by Stacks. She brought herself to a climax thinking to herself wondering how much money Sin gave Stacks to earn herself a fucking the way he was fucking her. Whatever it was she knew she had to work extra hard in the future because she wanted to be blessed with the dick the same way he was giving it to Sin.

After Stacks and Sin had sex, Sin curled up saying to herself 'now I know why the rest of the girls amongst themselves called him 'Mr. Dick Em' Down Good.' She wanted to savor the moment so she slipped into a deep sleep realizing that it would be a long time before, if ever again, she would be blessed with some dick that good because it was a known fact amongst the girls that Stacks rarely, if ever, fucked any of the girls more than once.

Noon came around faster than Stacks planned because the phone woke him up.

"Hello!"

"Good afternoon this is the front desk. Will you be staying another night?"

"Yes! I will be staying over but I'll be keeping just one of the suites; the one that I am currently in at this present moment. I'll be sending the money down in a few minutes."

"Thank you sir," replied the man at the front desk.

"Sin, wake up and go next door and wake Summer up. Then bring all the bags over here when you finish. Take this down to the front desk for another night even though we will be leaving later on sometime today," said Stacks.

Stacks handed her just enough money to pay for the room; no more, no less. "Ok Stacks." Stacks got in the shower and got dressed. Then Sin and Summer took turns taking a shower.

"Yo put a rush on getting ready because at three o-clock we out of here with or without Mandy," said Stacks. Three o-clock came, Stacks turned the key in, and tipped the bell hop to load the truck up. Sin and Summer were in the truck listening to an R&B mix CD, that Summer got the night before from one of her clients who was a DJ, when Mandy came running up to the truck all excited.

"Stacks! I have a Russian multi-millionaire on my line checking for me!" said Mandy.

"Bitch! I could care less about whose on your line for you. You could have the white boy who run the playboy mansion himself on your line. Where the fuck my money at hoe?"

That's when she reached in her coach hand bag and pulled out a wad of money and asked for the platter. Stacks told her to just drop it on the front seat. After she did what she was told to do she then told Stacks that the Russian wanted to deposit a half million dollars into his account to "let her go."

"What you mean let you go?"

"I mean he wants me for himself. I told him that the only way you'll let me go is if he would be able to wire half a million dollars into your account. I'm not really trying to stay with him.

I just want to get that money for you because that will put you ahead of the game."

"When is he trying to do this?"

"Right now; he is in the lobby waiting on my answer."

"Go tell him I'll be right in to discuss business with him. As for you let me explain something to you about tricking and lying to a muthafucka that's willing to pay that much money for some artificial love. It puts you on the edge of life. If he does this, then you'll have to stay with him for at least long enough so that he won't feel like the sucka he really is," said Stacks.

"I know that Stacks, but he is trying to wife me and take me back to his country and right now. I am not trying to be a wife to nobody. He says as soon as we are married he can put a speedy process on my passport so we can leave for Russia," said Mandy.

"Alright let's go see this muthafucka."

Once inside Stacks sat down with the Russian who was accompanied by bodyguards. They discussed the business then Stacks opened his laptop while the Russian made the transfer. Right before Stacks' eyes he watched a half of million dollars appear. Mandy had went outside to say her goodbyes to Sin and Summer. Then Stacks came out gave Mandy a slight devilish grin and told her that everything was final and told her to "get the fuck away" from his hoes and "go get a life with that Russian muthafucka."

Chapter 6

The P.O. Set Up

The Cadillac truck moved casually into the driveway. Stacks parked in front of the estate. As if on cue, Tequila came running out of the house and right into his arms.

"Hello Stacks!" she said overly excited. "Are you not surprised to see me?"

"Calm down Tequila," he said calmly.

Sin and Summer stood there with a shocked expression on their face, not knowing who this woman was that Stacks was now walking back into the house with.

Stacks turned around and told Sin and Summer to bring everything into the house. Once in the house he noticed Winter was standing off to the right. He then gave orders to her to go help with the bags as he went straight into the basement with Tequila.

"So what's up Tequila?"

"Nothing Stacks. I been waiting for you to come home so I could spend some quality time with you," said Tequila.

"Well let's get one thing straight," said Stacks.

"What's that?"

"Life for me on this side is much more intense when it comes to me making money. I don't mix wine with milk, in other words my business always come first to me no matter what. The way I carry myself holds a lot of weight when it comes to me being a hoe boss. I know how emotional you can get. First and foremost you're going to have to understand that whatever I do or tell you to do is for the betterment of this establishment. It's like Beanie Sigel said in one of his songs 'if you get your team right that's the green light to get your green right.' Are you sure you ready for this type of lifestyle?"

"Yes, I'm sure, as long as I'm with you making you happy. I'm ready for whatever I owe you a great deal for opening my eyes up to a life that I thought only existed on a movie screen, especially growing up in such a small town like Leavenworth Kansas."

"Well as long as you fuck with my pimpin' and realize that I am your lucky charm you will forever have access to that pot of gold at the end of the rainbow. Now get upstairs and get ready for the meeting tonight."

"Ok Stacks!"

"And one other thing. Where is my cuzzin' Precious at?" said Stacks.

"She said that she had a few errands to run and that she will meet you at the club about ten tonight."

Stacks dialed K's cell phone and he picked up instantly. "Bleed I'm at the house, where you at?"

"I'm in traffic headed to the house to take a shower. I just left Ferguson park shooting hoops with them Hilltop Cliffview O.G.s."

"Who you talking about?" said Stacks.

"That nigga Throw-down, Big Mooch, and Macka-doshish, along with a few other off-brand ass niggas," said K.

"Well, I need you to follow me so I can drop this rental off at the airport."

"Cool bleed, I'll be there in about an hour after I freshen' up."

"Alright my nigga I'll holla at you," said Stacks as he hung up.

An hour later K pulled up in a black Audi and followed Stacks to the airport. Once they dropped the rental off, on their way back they engaged in a conversation about Stacks' probation officer, Mr. Malone.

"So what did you find out about my PO?" said Stacks.

"Oh yeah, I had one of my workers follow him the other day and come to find out owe boy Mr. Malone is a dick sucking faggot. He goes to that dominatrix spot over on 30th and Payne. When he left, my guy put his gorilla down on the receptionist and was able to liberate the security DVD recording of his session taking dick in his back while swallowing cum juice."

"Dam! I knew something was up with that bitch ass muthafucka. So were the DVD at?" said Stacks.

"It's in the glove compartment. I got like three copies of them muthafuckas. Stacks looked in the glove compartment and saw that it was only two in there.

"Bleed it's only two copies in here."

"Oh yeah my worker broke into Mr. Malone's car and left a copy for him to see. That way when you go to report Monday you can have something to talk about," said K. They both laughed.

"And here is his address to where he live at with his wife and four kids."

"Now that's what I'm talking about bleed, come Monday morning it's going to be a lot of changes to my supervised release! Ok now that, that is out of the way; what about the carwash because I'm not going to be needing them check stubs anymore now that I am in possession of this DVD."

"It's a green light on the carwash. He said to give him eighty thousand for the spot and he will use the 20 we gave him and put towards the asking price; which is one hundred thousand. And as for him keeping employment he won't be doing that because he said he is tired of the business anyway. He said he is going to move his family down south in Florida to a beach house he owns," said K.

"Well all of that sounds good because later on today my C.P.A will be flying in from Cali so I'll have her to handle that business when she touch down. Also my other bitch that is an R.N., plus a national fitness personal trainer, will be coming as well. So I am going to need you to pick both of them up from the airport. Their plane lands at 9:00 tonight," said Stacks.

"I got you big hommie," replied K.

"Alright then drop me off at the house and I'll see you later on at the meeting. I have to get me some sleep so that a pimp can be on point tonight at the meeting."

The meeting was held later on that evening. Winter, Sin, Summer, Tequila, and Carmella all piled into a stretch Hummer along with Stacks, who was dressed up in the "flyest" gear that money could buy. They were headed to Precious' club called: 'Bottoms Up' on the East side of the 'Flats.'

Bottoms Up was a three story club that was part hip-hop, part reggae, and two part strip club. On the first floor was the hip-hop and reggae club and upstairs was where the male dancers entertained the women. Then you had to go to the basement to discover where the club got its name.

There was ass and tits everywhere. This is where all the "trickin'" and "hoeing" went on. Once inside Stacks and his hoes went straight to the bottom all the way to the VIP section where Precious was at with two hoes that Stacks had never seen before.

"Hey big cuzz what's up with you looking all fly tonight?" asked Precious.

"Well you know me I stay fresh dressed and ready to impress, sipping sweet honey, and counting major cash money. Who are these two honeys?" Stacks asked as he turned facing the chicks that were with Precious.

"Oh this is Peaches and her sister Cream."

"Hello ladies what's up with the two of you?"

"Hello Stacks," one of the girls said. Then the other one said, "Well to our understanding, from what Precious was telling us, you have a couple of slots open and we were wandering if you would let us fill them slots?"

"The only thing I need filled are my pockets so if you are ready to invest in my pockets like the mutha-fucking stock market then that's another topic because my choosing fee is ten thousand a piece or shall I say ten a key because the game I'm selling is raw and uncut; 100% pimpin, simp free - when you fucking with me, so what's it gone be? You gone get down and hoe down?"

"Of course we gone make it do what it do. It's only logic that we choose you."

Peaches & Cream were identical twins of Jamaican & Moroccan descent. The both of them stood about 5 feet tall with big breasts, a small waist, and a fat ass you could set a drink on top of. They both had greenish blue eyes that set on a round face with hair down to their banging hips and ass with a honey roasted peanut skin tone. They were a mixture of Nia long with the touch of Alissa Milliano. The only difference was a tiny Mole that set on Cream's right cheek.

Stacks took a step back and looked the both of them up and down spinning them around then said, "As soon as the meeting is over I want the both of you to immediately go do what you do best and get my mutha fucking money. Now let's head to the back and get this meeting in order."

"What's up everybody? I called this meeting tonight so that everyone can get acquainted with one another. So look around the room and introduce yourselves. I need everybody in here to understand that everybody in here has a part to play in this establishment. Understand your part and your part only; so that way you may be the best at what you do. Now there are a few major things that I would like to touch base on. First and foremost is that the only muthafuckas that give orders around here is me, my balls, and my words. The second most important thing is if I find out that you - and that means everybody in here - are ever caught stealing my money or not breaking yourself of all your earnings, then prepare to become famous because I'm gone make your ass famous by putting these 'Hollywoods on your Ass!" Stacks said as he held up his fist.

"So much that when I am done beating your ass you gone think that you are on the Hollywood walk of fame from all the stars your ass gone be seeing because I am going to beat your ass black & blue. So don't steal from me and always remember that the word loyalty is more than just a seven letter word; which brings me to saying that if you come across another pimp drop your head and keep walking without saying a word. Treat him like he is the negative side of a magnet and that you are the positive. The closer he get, the further you go to get away from his ass. Reckless eyeballing is for renegade ass hoes. Carry yourself like you a seasoned bitch trying to get rich.

"You see everybody's success will come from following my commandments. Make my vision your vision. The number one goal is for everyone to help me help you all so you all can continue to help me. If I am happy then you all will be happy. So keep me happy that way you all will remain happy. There is no limit to what you all can do. Respect the game and the game will respect you.

"Jealousy, envy, hoe hating and deceit are the wrong characteristics to have because they can destroy this empire. Truthfulness, loyalty, honor and respect, along with selflessness on you all's part is what will take us above and beyond the land of milk and honey.

"Also, when it comes to turning a date always get the person to indulge in some type of sexual physical contact before they give you any money because one thing that the police or the Fed's cannot do is touch you in a sexual way. Also, always ask if they have any affiliations with the police or the Fed's to make sure they are not confidential informants.

"As for those who have cops as clients this does not apply to you. If by any chance you get picked up for questioning or if you get arrested keep my name or anybody else's name that is a part of this household out your mouth because death is waiting for you around the corner and will meet you head on if you run your mouth. Just know that I do have police, politicians, as well as county workers on my pay roll now. If you don't want to become yesterday's paper or a remunerable thought, it will be to your advantage if you be patient, then call Precious and explain the situation and she will be the one to get you out.

"As you may see in front of you there are cell phones and this is how you will communicate. These phones are strictly for business, so that means no personal calls. Tomorrow morning the photographer will be by to do a photo shoot of everyone as a group then there will be single shots of each and every one of you. The photographer will also be taking an additional five pictures that will be duplicated to be circulated throughout the prison system. I will be posting these pictures on the internet throughout different sites. From this day forth you all will be working under my company name known as 'Stacks Doll Babies.'

"You all will be doing private parties, single, and double dates. Monday morning each and every one of you will go register with the state as a certified hoe," Stacks said as he started laughing.

"Naw, I'm just playing. Your registration will be for you to be an escort, entertainer, as well as a professional model. You will keep your license on you at all times. I have an exclusive list of clients that range from all around the world who will also be shown your pictures. So remember the better you look the better your chances will be to be chosen for the big money spenders.

"As for your clients it is important that you all learn your client's likes and dis-likes. Never wear the same outfit twice on a date with the same person, unless that outfit is requested by your client. Always make sure your hair is done as well as your nails. Hygiene is top priority and professionalism is a key factor to remain successful in this game. So always look your best.

"You are the product that you are attempting to sell. Referrals are what you are looking for from your client's besides his or her money. Tina here is a registered nurse, as well as a national fitness personal trainer, so she will be giving you a HIV test, as well as any other venereal disease test. So if you get infected just know that your contract with this establishment is voided instantly. So protect yourself at all times. I need money, not an infected ass bitch!

"Mondays, Wednesdays, and Saturdays for one hour will be a mandatory cardio and calisthenics class. This will add definition to them curves. Tina has also took the time out, upon my request, to make a nutritional menu that everyone will follow. I need you all to become the sexist bitches on the planet.

"Last, but not least, please know that no matter how many tricks you fuck, you can never run out of pussy. You will always have enough pussy left to sell."

Stacks poured everybody a drink and held his goblet up and said "Blind, cripple, or crazy - keep on hoeing and don't be lazy! Pimp, pimp, hoeray today is a hoeley day! You all have been blessed by the best the pimp-king himself!"

Monday morning Stacks walked into Mr. Malone's with an extra side of confidence. As soon as he walked in he noticed two plain clothes white males that looked like two undercover detectives, who actually turned out to be just that.

"Hello Mr. Stacks my name is detective Mills. Can you please come with us? We would like to question you in reference to a female by the name of Amanda Brown. She was last seen with you checking into a Detroit hotel that was registered in your name."

The two detectives escorted Stacks across the street to the city jail and placed him in an interrogation room. Once inside the room, the second detective sat down in a chair directly across from Stacks then said "My name is detective Smith, I am the head detective on this case. I was just wondering how is it that your name is Stacks Money? Is that the name that your parents gave you?"

"Naw, I changed my name when I turned 21 and before I answer any other questions I would like to call my lawyer."

"If you don't have anything to hide then why is that you need a lawyer? You're not under arrest as of yet," said detective Smith.

"Well, if I am not under arrest then open the door and let me the fuck out of here!"

"Well, I wish it was that easy. But it's not. Take a look at this picture," said the detective.

Stacks grabbed the Detroit Press and read the front page: 'A female was found in a downtown hotel room and was identified as Amada Brown from Cleveland, Ohio.'

"So what does that have to do with me?"

"It has a lot to do with you. You see we have you on camera checking into the same hotel that she was murdered at with her and two other females. But the day you were leaving you were seen leaving only with two of the females that you checked in with. Then discussing some type of business with this guy here in the lobby." Then the detective showed Stacks a picture of the Russian guy.

"That guy there, that you are looking at, is a member of the Russian mafia so we assume that you are trafficking women since that is the line of business that he is in."

"Man, fuck you! That bitch! And that Russian mafia muthafucka! I don't have shit else to say to you except that I want to call my lawyer." Stacks called his lawyer then within twenty minutes his lawyer, Kanisha Love, appeared demanding that her client be released. Since he was not being charged for anything, he was released to the custody of his probation officer.

"Mr. Stacks what do you have to say for yourself about violating your probation by leaving the state without permission. You know I can send you back to prison for what you have done and your lawyer that's out there waiting on you would not be able to do a dam thing for you?"

"I totally understand that Mr. Malone, but you might want to rethink that before you do that because I can totally destroy your career, marriage, and good ole wholesome life of yours," said Stacks. "Now how would you do that?" said Mr. Malone.

"Let me ask you something Mr. Malone?"

"And what would that be?"

"When was the last time you were on 30th and Payne?"

"What are you trying to say?" said Mr. Malone.

"I am pretty sure you know exactly what the fuck I am talking about you dick sucking ass faggot. You are a poor excuse for a man - a straight up fag. Now let me explain something to you about how shit will be operated for the remainder of my eleven months on probation. I am not submitting anymore urine and as for me reporting once a month - that's out the equation. The next time I want to hear from you is when my probation is over and you are faxing over my release papers to my lawyer. Now if you disagree to the things that I am saying, then what you are telling me is that you don't mind the DVD of you involved in homosexual acts being posted on YouTube or showing up on every coworker of your's desk. Not to mention me sending a copy to your wife as well as all your children's teachers."

"Ok, ok enough, I get the message just promise me that this never leaves this office." "You got my word," said Stacks who stood up then said, "Have a nice day."

Chapter 7

Vanity Wash

It had been six months since Mandy's death and Stacks had rearranged his supervised release with his probation officer. He now had the carwash doing big numbers. He turned a regular carwash into the "flyest" spot in the city of Cleveland to be at when it came to getting your carwash and making it rain on the strippers. It was a 24hr spot were all the big names hung around. Every-body that was somebody came from everywhere - even out of state.

Money getters were partaking in the accommodations that were being offered at the carwash. He sold beer, liquor, and wine during regular business hours and turned the lower level of the carwash into an 'after hour' joint. He had a stage built for the strippers to perform when they weren't washing the cars and provided whatever your money could afford. He installed private booths on the lower level.

It had to be the first of its kind. Truthfully speaking, there was no other place like it. The place was called 'Vanity Wash.' Bitches from everywhere on the map were auditioning to work for Stacks. He eventually started his own magazine called 'Bitches.' He now had a carwash, a website full of hoes going on exclusive expensive dates with "A" list clients; which consisted of doctors, lawyers, policemen, judges, drug king pens, and Mafia made men.

Stacks even served an employee from the United States House of Representative who would have Winter meet him every time that he traveled out of the country. He would have a five star hotel waiting on her.

Stacks also had the hot shots circulating throughout the American prison system, the Chinese prison system, and three European countries. So with all of that and his Doll House, that he invested in on the outskirts of Las Vegas, Stacks had accumulated a little over a million dollars in the bank. He bought himself a custom brick and stone manor estate in Houston, Texas with a seven car garage, ten bathrooms, a heated pool, a built in theater, and a full court gym. The estate sat on nine point seven acres of land for three million dollars.

He spent another $980,000 on a custom made bullet proof diamond black fully loaded ultra-rare drop head Mabach 62 landaulet with a cocaine white interior. He also had three lp560 Lamborghinis in three different colors at $280,000 a piece for his top three cum catching hoes Sin, Summer, and Tequila. The rest of the bitches got chauffeured around except for the twins, Peaches and Cream. They had this billionaire from Arabia who would fly them in once a month for the weekend to Las Vegas. He would give them both $100,000 dollars apiece just to be his personal slaves. So stacks bought them both triple pink 68

Shelby Mustangs GT500 convertibles because they stayed faithful and they earned it!

Stacks had been staying in Houston Texas with his starting lineup Carmella, Sin, Summer, Winter, Tequila, Peaches, and Cream. They all stayed at the fortress and operated from Houston now.

Stacks went back in Ohio to meet with K. He bought Winter along. Tequila wanted to come but she had to fly to Germany and meet this major of the United States Army. If Obama only knew how one of his top majors spent his money on a certified hoe.

K sent the car to pick Stacks and Winter up from the airport. The driver was "LA," a cold-blooded killer from Detroit who took on the name LA after he wiped out a crew from LA. That crew was selling drugs on another drug dealing crew's territory called the "Cheddar Boyz."

LA was dating a girl by the name of Diamond who was the cuzzin' of one of the Cheddar Boyz. So LA and his crew annihilated the crew from LA one night after a shootout at Scandaler Park (the name of the park is really Chandler Park but it adapted its name Scandaler for being so scandalous).

The shootout that occurred between the Cheddar Boyz and the LA Crew took Diamond's life from a bullet to the head. Stacks met LA in Leavenworth. LA was serving a 36 month sentence for a gun charge and told him to look him up when he got out.

"LA! What up bleed?"

"What up dough big-money Stacks? How you doing tonight?"

"Man it's all good. How you like my establishment at the carwash?"

"Man it took a genius to come up with an idea like that, I mean who would have thought to turn a carwash into a 24 hour seven days a week strip club. A place where you can get your car washed and at the same time watch those bitches get wet while they stripping all the same time. Then the private do whatever your money can afford booths in the lower level is a for real money getter as well!"

Stacks slipped into a deep thought thinking how the carwash was doing big numbers.

"Stacks!" Winter called out breaking his train of thought. "Are you okay?"

"Yeah! Why you ask?"

"Because he just asked you a question."

"Oh, what up LA?" said Stacks.

OG Stack$

"What I was asking was do you know some guy by the name of Shakim? He said he is from New York City. He just came to the spot about two hours ago saying he needs to see you."

"Oh yeah, word! The God Shakim at the spot. Who did he come with?" said Stacks.

"Nobody as far as I know. Do I need to body that nigga or is he good?" said LA.

"Oh yeah that's my homeboy from Brownsville we used to do business together bleed, okay."

Once they arrived at the Vanity Wash, Stacks and Winter went straight to Stacks' office upstairs where he could see everything go on through a tinted bulletproof window.

"Yo Winter! You see that guy right there with a black leather coat?"

"Yeah I see him."

"Go tell him to come here and show him how to get upstairs. Then go hit the dressing room & put something sexy on and walk the floor to see if you can find out from the other girls if any of them been pocketing my money off the top."

"Will do Stacks, but I don't think any of the girls are holding out," said Winter.

"Bitch! I didn't tell you to think. I told you to go walk the muthafucking floe hoe. Make me think you stealing my money!"

"I would never do that daddy."

"Well then beat yo feet on the concrete and go find out!"

A few minutes later Shakim came walking into the office. "Peace to the God. What up nature?"

"Yo! Maintaining my cipher God but address me as Stacks around here. These 85ers don't know I reign supreme with the knowledge of self!" said Stacks.

"What you doing in the land? The word back home is that you on some pimpin' shit; holding shit down out of town with a bunch of clowns. Yo name screaming in the streets since you hit the bricks that you living the life of the savage chasing after the cabbage. Being that you are part of the Nation of Gods and Earths yo name came up at the Parliament. But you know we all fall off our square," said Shakim.

"So what's the science. What is it you trying to say. How did you even know Stacks was me nature?" said Stacks.

"You know the God Divine?" replied Shakim.

"Yeah I know the God Divine. He doing a life bit upstate for snuffing that kid Smokey and he rocked EM to sleep into a permanent dirt nap. Yeah that's Sun. What about him?" asked Stacks.

"Yo his BM work for you as one of your dancers. As a matter of fact she downstairs right now. Her name is Akelia."

"Oh yeah shorty from the Bronx started working for me about two weeks ago. She say she used work at Sin City, so what's the beef?"

"Naw there's no beef. He just asked me if you could like keep an eye on her because he has his seed with her."

"Yeah no doubt you got my word. Also I am trying to eat with you Kid," said Shakim.

"Yo I'm going to keep it 100 with you right now. I'm dwelling in the triple stages of darkness but I am shining like the light in the night and I'm not trying to let up so don't expect me to be right and exact standing on my square," said Stacks.

"Naw, Naw Sun, do you. I just need to be able to breathe easy."

"All right then the first thing I need to know is do you have your driver's license?"

"Yeah! I'm valid."

"Cool I am going to put you behind a wheel as a driver and a personal bodyguard to all my bitches. The only thing is that you cannot be resurrecting the dead with all that God body and Queen mother Earth talk to my hoes. I can't have none of my bitches waking up and thinking for them self because if my bitches start using their brain then they might go crazy from realizing how dumb, deaf, and blind they have been."

Stacks and Shakim began laughing.

"Drive and keep your mouth shut and if you want to fuck any of my bitches it's going to cost you because don't none of my bitches smoke crack so the pussy is not free! You can live in the guest house with the rest of the guys. Oh yeah that kid LA, he's a straight goon so fall back because he is the head of my security."

"I got you stacks."

"All right I get at you later. Peace!" said Stacks.

Stacks cell phone went off and he quickly answered knowing that it was K calling. "What up?" answered Stacks.

"Hey stacks where you at? Yo I'm at the wash where you at?"

"I just left a business meeting with this music producer. He said that he needed to use five of your chicks for a video shoot.

He got this new artist from West Virginia that is burning up the airwaves."

"Yeah I heard about some new kid named Nonchalant. He is supposed to be real smooth with his flows," said Stacks.

"I will be at the carwash in about 10 minutes," said K.

"Alright that's cool that way I can fax the paperwork over to my lawyer and she can go over the contracts," said Stacks.

"Man Stacks you need a business lawyer not a criminal lawyer! What the fuck you think she is; the bitch does it all! And I mean does it all!"

"I bet you didn't know I been breaking that bitches husband's bank account. Ever since she had my son 10 months before I got locked up. When I was on the inside we took a DNA test and little dude is my flesh and blood. Her husband know all about it but didn't file for divorce because a year before she had my son he got his secretary pregnant and she took it on the chin like a champ," said Stacks.

"So you mean to tell me that your son lives with another man?

"Hell naw nigga! She don't live with that nigga no more. Her and my son live in Hudson, Ohio."

"Yeah! What is his name?"

"What you think nigga? His name is Young Money. First name Young, last name Money just like his daddy Stacks. Money where do you think that I've been going to three days out of the month?" said Stacks.

"What are you saying, that she is your wife?" said K.

"Look nigga don't you ever disrespect a pimp like that. She's just my bitch, my son's mother, and the only bitch that I am not trying to pimp! Yo K, I'm out."

"Cool I'll see you when I get there, peace," said K.

Fifteen minutes later "K" arrived and Stacks went straight to the topic on his mind.

"K, I spoke to Moet the other day and she was explaining to me that the Fed's was not going to renew the contract for the program. She said they were shutting down a lot of programs including Unicore. So what I was going to do was send all the females from the program down to Las Vegas to the Doll House and I would like you to move down there with Precious. The Doll House is already good doing numbers. I just need somebody I can trust living on the property that's familiar with the way I want things to be ran."

"Yeah! That would be a good move. I just don't know if Precious is for something like that being the fact that she is just now getting her strip club all the way off the ground," replied K.

OG Stack$

"Well that's no problem because Precious is going to ride or die for me on whatever plus I am going to give her a million dollars so that she can expand her strip club in Las Vegas as a token of my appreciation for doing this job," said Stacks.

"I am all in but I need a favor from you bro," asked K.

"Anything, you just name it and it's yours."

"Well, my favor is that I want Sin," said K.

"Oh! You like Sin huh?" said Stacks.

"Actually I don't, it's your cousin. Her and Sin has been at it for months. They just didn't know how to tell you."

"Now that is a different story," said Stacks. "You are taking money out of my pocket. The bitch makes me good money. I tell you what I am going to do. I'm gonna give you that million dollars to start the club, with a 10% interest rate, along with 30% ownership. Then you and Precious can do as you both please with that bitch."

"Let me talk things over with Precious first, then I'll get back at you with a decision."

"This is a now or never deal. You work whatever is needed to be worked out with Precious on your time. So what is your answer? If you smart you will jump on board with what I am saying and put that little Asian bitch to work so you can cash me out," said Stacks.

"All right Stacks you got a deal," replied K.

"Then it's official. I'll put Sin on a plane first thing smoking as soon as you both get to Vegas. Come on, let's go pop a bottle to seal the deal."

When Stacks and K got downstairs by the bar Precious came walking in looking like a million bucks. Stacks thought to himself if Precious wasn't his cousin that she would be one fine piece of pussy to put on the market. She had her hair in a Mohawk with the sides waved up. Her skin looked extra creamy tonight like she soaked her whole body in a ton of shay butter; it was flawless. She wore a pair of blue diamond earrings with a matching necklace, she was rocking a royal blue chinchilla. Her breasts were firm and were looking like two coconuts. The sexy lace blue Armani tight fitting dress she had on was hugging every curve on her video vixen body. She was looking like she just walked up out of a rap video.

Then, as if it was planned, the song "I'm bossy" came on as she walked over to where Stacks and K were sitting and drinking. She was the center of attraction.

"Dam Precious what's the special occasion?" asked Stacks, referring to her captivating appearance.

"Why does it have to be a special occasion because a boss bitch like myself wants to turns heads tonight?"

"Which nigga head you trying to turn?" questioned K.

"Whichever one of these week ass niggas in here that's gonna get down like he live and put some money in my purse. Is not that the way it goes Big Cuzz? 'Purse first, ass last,' although unlike these dumb ass hoes, I don't have to fuck or suck a niggas dick to get my money. I make a soft nut nigga pay me just for my time and to have an arm piece like me to be seen with him."

"So now you pimpin' like yo cuzzin' hun?" asked K.

"No I'm not pimpin' I am just playing my position and getting all the game I can. That way I can use my mouth piece the way he taught me."

"Fall back Precious and check yo-self when you in the presence of a pimp. Because cuzzin' or no cuzzin' you still got a slit with a clit so don't be poppin' that slick shit around me. I blessed you with game to stay up on a lame, not my hommie K."

"Well if he act like a lame then I am going to treat him like one. He know that he is the only sweet daddy long dick I need in my life I am not fucking nobody but him."

"Yeah! And don't you forget to mention one of my hoes," said Stacks.

"Who are you talking about, Sin? I pay well for that pussy every time she wrapped her legs around my head and it's worth every dollar. I tried to sleep with her for free but she didn't want to disappoint her 'dick-em down good daddy Stacks' as she say."

"Look precious I was just going over a few things with K and I have a proposition for you; where we all will be able to come out on top."

"What's that Stacks?" said Precious.

"What you think about moving to Vegas and opening up a second club?"

"Don't you own property out there?" asked Precious.

"Actually, I do. I have a full blown establishments going on at the present moment and I figured since you spending money on Sin I am going to let you have the bitch as long as you agree to moving out there with K and run things according to the way me and K just discussed. K will explain everything in detail later on," said Stacks.

"Well, as long as I get to sit at table and eat then I'm good," replied Precious.

"I got you. It's enough money for everybody to eat."

Stacks poured her a drink, she accepted the drink then Stacks, K and Precious held their glasses up and while Stacks made a toast and said "Here's to hoes, tricks, and moneymaking pimps." They all sat back and drank until the sun came up. Then Winter came over and approached Stacks.

"Daddy, can we go? The sun is up and I have a 8 o'clock appointment with a regular. I would like to take a bath and freshen up."

"Okay let me go and get LA, then we can leave," said Stacks.

CHAPTER 8

Winter and Garvin

"It's 8 o'clock. Where is he at?" said Winter, pacing back and forth as she spoke to Stacks.

"Maybe you should give him a call and make sure that he's still coming," said Stacks.

"I cannot do that because he lives with his wife and when he calls me he always calls private so I don't have his number."

Winter's phone start buzzing so she anxiously picked it up. "Hello!" said Winter.

"Hello lovely. This is Garvin. I know I am running a little late but I am pulling up as we speak. I had an emergency at the hospital last night. The late night surgeon is at home with the flu so they called me in to perform an emergency surgery on a young man who needed to have the whole right side of his face reconstructed after he had been shot in the face three times. But I intend to make being late up to you while we are in Miami."

"Did you say Miami?" said Winter.

"Yes Miami. What you think about a two day vacation with full access to my black card?"

"Ummmm, that sounds very interesting."

"So what is that, a yes?"

"Of course that is a yes."

"Okay then come on out so that we can catch our plane. It leaves at 9 o'clock and we have no time to waste."

"Okay Garvin, please allow me grab my overnight bag and I'll be right out," said Winter before she ended the call.

"Daddy he is outside and he wants to take me to Miami for a couple of days."

"Bitch, I don't give a fuck if he wanted to take you from here to Jamaica. As long as when you get back you got my mutha fucking paper and stay up on top of your game while representing my name," said Stacks.

"Aww daddy that's an automatic for me I'm your number one team player. I will see you when I get back," said Winter.

"Yeah whatever," replied Stacks.

A few hours later they arrived in Miami and jumped in the limo that Garvin had waiting on them.

"Garvin, I would like to go shopping before we get to the hotel," Winter said.

"We're not staying at a hotel. I have a condo on Fisher Island. You'll love it - I promise. I want to go to the strip club later on tonight and explore our options for a threesome."

"Ok!"

"Driver take us to Bal-Harbor."

Three hours later with over $25,000 of some of the most expensive name brands in clothes, hand bags, as well as shoes she was ready to go; after she made one last stop at Ventura Mall. Winter picked out Stacks a platinum diamond pinky ring in the design of a dollar sign symbol, which came to $75,000.

As they were pulling up to the condo, Winter noticed a 911 RuF Ctr3 Porsche that sat in the driveway.

"Are you expecting somebody?" asked Winter.

"No! Why would you ask that?" replied Garvin.

"Because there is a Porsche in the driveway. Oh I get it! This is where you bring all your females to seduce them huh?"

"No! This is where my wife and I, for the last ten years, have been coming since the first time I bought it. I told you that I love my wife, it's just ever since you came in to the hospital to get your breast implants, you are making it hard for me to stay married."

"There is nothing wrong with having a chick on the side," said Winter.

"That's why I like spending time with you, there is never a dull moment with you. Come on let me show you the inside."

Garvin and the limo driver unloaded the bags. Winter stood in the middle of the entrance admiring the setup of the condo.

"So how do you like it?" asked Garvin.

"Oh it's beautiful! Where is the bathroom? I want to go pamper my face."

"It's upstairs in the main bedroom or you can use the one over there to the right."

"I rather use the upstairs' one," said Winter.

"Ok, then go ahead on up and I'll be down here fixing something to eat. I'm starving."

"Me too baby, make something light," replied Winter.

"How about a couple of turkey sandwiches with a bowl of salad?"

"That'll do."

Winter grabbed her overnight bag then went upstairs. When she finished she came back downstairs where Garvin was sitting on an Italian leather couch watching a 42 inch plasma. She sat down next to him then began eating her food. Afterwards he took the remainder of food into the kitchen and Winter followed him.

"Garvin did you bring my weed with you? You know how it relaxes me," said Winter.

"I didn't bring any because there is some already here upstairs next to the bed in a glass jar. I'm going up to make myself comfortable don't keep me waiting honey."

She got upstairs and saw the weed jar on the edge of the bed. She rolled a nice phat blunt, sparked it up then laid back sitting up on the bed. She grabbed the remote then start flicking through the channels. Garvin came in and started removing his clothes. He walked in the bathroom and got in the shower leaving the door open so Winter can see him take a shower through the glass shower door.

After a few puffs on the blunt she went over to pour herself a glass of some Red Velvet Nuvo that was sitting on top of the miniature refrigerator where she also grabbed an ice cube to put in her drink. Then she sat back on the bed and waited for Garvin to finish up in the shower. By the time he came out of the shower, she had a light buzz from the drink she had drunk along with the weed she was smoking.

Garvin came out of the bathroom totally naked and took the blunt from Winter. Then he grabbed the sensual massage oil out of the drawer and handed the oil to Winter to rub onto his 6'2 225 pound frame of solid muscles. She started rubbing the oil onto him as he stood. He had a full erection. He then climbed into the bed, laid down on his back and she straddled him without putting his dick in her. He palmed her ass while she continued to rub the oil on his chest placing light kisses on his neck, chest, and then his lips. Then they began kissing passionately. He could feel her warm juices from her dripping wet pussy on her body.

She leaned down to find his dick standing at full attention; leaned over like the Eiffel Tower. She slowly started sucking his dick at the tip going extra slow making circular motions around his dick head. It was swelling by the constant sucking she was doing. As she eased his whole dick into her mouth, while holding it in her hand going up and down on it massaging it with her hand, she started deep throating him. He was moaning from the pleasures she was giving him as his dick was on the edge of exploding. She continued to swallow his manhood as he looked at her, amazed at how good she was sucking his dick. She had sucked his dick before, but never with this much passion.

She was rubbing her clit while playing with her pussy as he was squeezing her nipples. She then straddled him again but this time grabbing his dick and positioning it as she slid down on it. Her pussy was so wet that his ten inches slowly disappeared into her deep walls of ecstasy. He began moaning and whispering, "Winter, dam this pussy is good ooooh my god." By now she was bouncing up and down on him. She was popping her pussy back and forth on his dick like she was on stage stripping at the club. He continued to say how good the pussy was.

She then said, "Dam this dick is good! Get this pussy daddy." Then her ass started shaking. She bit her bottom lip as she could feel him exploding inside of her. "Oooh Garvin! I'm cumming." Then she came as his still hard dick was still pumping upward. Then he turned her over and entered her from the back in the doggy style position.

She was shouting, "Fuck me Garvin! Please fuck me harder pleeeeasse I want all of you in me!" He went deeper and deeper as he pushed all ten inches into her. The more he pounded, the more that pussy opened up. She was screaming at the top of her lungs. He then shoved her face into the pillow to muffle the screams, moans, and grunts. He was fucking her fast and going deep smacking her on her ass. Her tits were bouncing back and forth. The more they fucked, the more they began to sweat. She was shaking from multiple orgasms which made him loose total control. He gripped her ass as he was exploding! Then they both collapsed onto the bed.

"Now that's what I call fucking," said Garvin.

"Ohh yes baby! You never fucked me like that before," replied Winter.

"Well, I never really had the time to take the time to put this dick up in you like I wanted to."

"Well, if you keep fucking me that good I'm going to have to move in with you and Mrs. Martin."

"Naw baby, if that pussy keep this dick cumming like it did tonight then I am going to have to move Mrs. Martin out and you in!" They both laughed.

Winter got up, went into the bathroom, turned the water on, got in the shower, and then Garvin joined in which led to them fucking for another hour playing shower games. After that Garvin dressed in an all-black Armani suite and put on a pair of "gators." He came down the stairs where Winter was waiting anxiously by the door. She had on a cream color Prada outfit with a pair of open toe Prada shoes.

"Why do you seem to be in such a rush?" asked Garvin.

"I am just ready to see some ass and titties shaking," replied Winter.

"Well, let's go and enjoy ourselves."

Once they got to the club and parked the car they noticed that line to get in was way down the street bending around the corner. Winter approached the doorman and told him that she had an appointment with the owner for an audition and that

Garvin was her personal bodyguard. So the doorman then let her and Garvin in the club.

The place was filled with half naked women some giving lap dances, others serving drinks, while the rest were dancing on all four stages.

"Winter! Winter is that you?" asked a chocolate thick Bowlegged girl.

"Dam you still look good girl. I haven't seen you since high school. What have you been doing?" asked the girl known as Pussy Cat.

"Hey Pussy Cat you don't look bad your dam self. Last I heard, you and Weezy was living in Atlanta. How is your sister doing?" asked Winter.

"That's her on stage over there."

"Wow! That's lil young ass Weezy Hun?" said Winter.

"Yeah, she all grown up. Who is your friend?" asked Pussy Cat.

"Oh, this is Garvin."

"Hello Miss Lady."

"Hello Garvin, please call me Pussy Cat."

"Ok, Pussy Cat, how are you doing tonight?"

"I'm good."

"How did you get the name Pussy Cat?" asked Garvin.

"They call her Pussy Cat cause she lick pussy like a cat lick its ass," said Winter. Both Winter and Pussy Cat started laughing.

"Garvin can you go get us a bottle of Ciroc so that I can have a few words with pussycat?"

"Ok I'll be back ladies," said Garvin.

"So pussycat what are you doing tonight?" asked Winter.

"Why do you ask?"

"I was just wondering if you would join me and Garvin tonight at his condo. That way I can see if that pussy still taste as sweet as she used to."

"Girl she might even taste better than that because I haven't had no dick since the last guy that beat me into a comma for two years."

"A comma?" asked Winter in a surprising way.

"Yeah, I was working the strip clubs when I was living in Atlanta and this pimp starting taking my money and beating my ass on a regular. So then one day I tried to fight him and he just commenced to beating the shit out of me. I mean, I respect the game of pimpin' - it's just I never met a pimp that did not have more than me, so I couldn't see giving my money to a muthafucka who had less than me."

"Dam baby you just caught a bad break because that's what a pimp is for. So that you won't get robbed and most definitely not beat, as long as you pay yo pimp and treat em like he yo man, you good he'll take care of you. I mean these streets are dangerous," said Winter.

"What you know about selling pussy? You got a man. One who looks like he love you dearly and you must love him just as much being the fact you trying to take me home as a treat."

"Girl allow me to explain something to you. I been selling pussy since we graduated from high school getting my ass beat by pimp after pimp until I met Stacks. I was a lost bitch in a cold hearted world," replied Winter.

"Stacks? I thought you said his name was Garvin?" said Pussy Cat.

"Garvin. I never said he was my man - you did. That nigga don't love me. He love how I make him feel mentally and physically. That's a trick ass nigga who is cheating on his wife; with a high priced hoe like me. Stacks is my pimp, he's my manager, who manages all my money, and he is my daddy cause he will only beat my ass when I do wrong and only because he care. He don't take my money.

"I give him my money, he feed me, cloth me, and give me shelter in about three different area codes. He is my God. I worship the ground he walk on and that nigga fucked me onetime like it was no tomorrow. Me and the rest of the girls call him 'Mr. Dick em down good' because whenever he put that dick on you, which is not that often, he puts it down and I have to admit he leaves a bitch begging for that sugar cane.

"I know one thing when I get back with the money I am making on this trip off this nigga, along with the ring I bought him, plus the outfits I got for the other girls, I'll be for sure to get blessed by the pimp king himself. He just loves it when we show love to one another. He say what you want for yourself you should want for your sister."

"Dam girl you talk like that nigga is all that," said Pussy Cat.

"Bitch! You must did not hear a word I said because that nigga all that and then some. Look at this," said Winter. She turned around and moved her hair to the side so that Pussycat could see the dollar sign tatted on the back of her neck then said "I am Stacks property and proud to be a part of the establishment. I live the life of a million dollar hoe because Stacks is a million dollar pimpin foe life ass nigga."

"So when can I meet this nigga because bitch I need some all that pimpin' in my life! Me and my sister's life!"

"Girl his pimpin isn't cheap. You need $10,000 just for him to hear you talk," replied Winter.

"Dam! Bitch what that nigga dick made of, gold?"

"Naw, it's platinum, but it's not the dick you paying for because you one lucky bitch if he even fuck you. It's his pimpin' and it is worth way more than that."

"Here you go ladies. As you requested a fresh bottle of Ciroc," said Garvin.

"Thank you baby," replied Winter.

"I hope you both had enough time to play catch up and that I am not disturbing you all."

"No, everything is ok baby," said Winter

"Pussycat give him a lap dance while I go make it rain on Weezy and see if she remembers me!"

Winter went to the stage where Weezy was putting on a show for the onlookers making her pussy blow smoke rings with the cigarette that she had in between her pussy lips.

"You go girl!" said Winter as she threw a stack of ones onto the stage. Weezy recognized Winter instantly and started smiling as she continued perform. Now she was on both of her knees making her ass cheeks jiggle from side to side. Winter looked over her shoulder and saw Pussycat doing her thang with Garvin. After the song went off, Weezy came off the stage and gave Winter a big hug.

"What's up Weezy?" said Winter.

"Nothing much girl. What you doing in Miami?" asked Weezy.

"I am out here on a business trip. The question is: how long have you been dancing?"

"For about a year. This plus amongst other things helps me and Pussy Cat pay bills. You know she is here with me," said Weezy.

"I know, she is over there giving my friend a lap dance. So where is it that you and Pussy Cat live at?"

"We stay in a hotel that's owned by the same that guy that own this club."

"I was talking to your sister about getting some real money."

"I'm in if she's in. Whatever it is it has to be better than this," said Weezy.

"Ok, then let's go get Pussy Cat." As they both walked up Pussy Cat was just finishing up with Garvin.

"So Pussy Cat what do you think about coming with me tonight and having some real fun?"

"What about me?" asked Wezzy.

"I tell you what, let's go to you all's room and grab your things," said Winter.

"Ok," replied Pussy Cat.

So they all left the club and headed over to the hotel room. They then went to Garvin's condo. That night Pussy Cat, Winter, and Garvin made out all night while Weezy relaxed in the comfort of his hot tub. Then she ended up falling asleep in the guest room.

Early the next morning Winter woke up and was downstairs cooking breakfast. Garvin came down and walked into the kitchen.

"Good morning sleepy head, how did you enjoy your night last night?" asked Winter.

"Thank you," said Garvin accepting the plate of cheese eggs and bacon with toast.

"Garvin! I need a big favor from you."

"And what's that lil momma?"

"I need you to help my girls out with some money," said Winter.

"That's no problem. How much are we talking?"

"Twenty thousand. I know that might be asking too much but it really means a lot to me if you can do this for me and help them."

"Are they in some type of trouble were the police may need to be involved?"

"No, it's not trouble or a problem. It's just they both had a bad break in life and I just wanted to lift the weight up off of their shoulders."

"Well, what about the twenty thousand I am supposed to be giving you for this trip?"

"Oh baby you know momma can't go home without that. Just look at it as a bonus for all the good work. Before you answer let me give you an incentive."

Then she got down on her knees and pushed Garvin back into the chair behind him pulled his dick out and began sucking his dick as he attempted to eat his breakfast, which was to no avail. Then out of nowhere Weezy walked in and saw Winter enjoying her breakfast, which looked like a chocolate stick with cream coming out of the top.

"Oh shit! Excuse me. Looks like I caught y'all at the wrong time," said Weezy.

"Actually! Your right on time, come on here and help me with making up his mind on giving you and your sister that money I said you guys needed last night at the hotel."

Weezy came over then slowly lowered her lips to Garvin's. Then she nibbled on his bottom lip briefly. This led to them to kissing each other with a very intense feeling between one another. She then straddled him and put his dick in her. He felt the wetness of her pussy being wrapped around his dick. She rested her upper body on his chest still kissing him she began moving up and down on his dick.

Winter was standing there watching Weezy tear into Garvin with such a sensual fuck. He palmed her ass as she rode his dick into an explosion.

"Dam you girls are dangerous the way y'all put that pussy on a nigga. How can I say no after something like that!" said Garvin.

Everybody laughed. Then Weezy and Winter both said "Thank you Garvin!" at the same time with such a devilish smile, that the devil himself would have been proud of, for the move they just put down.

Garvin said, "No. Thank you ladies because these last 24 hours have been some of the best moments in my life. I feel like

Stack$ ...pimpin' for life

I'm back in college at one of my fraternity parties. Then Weezy and Winter excused themselves and went upstairs to share some hot water in the shower together as Garvin followed behind to relax while he enjoyed his early morning coffee as he watched the news and transferred $40,000 over to the usual account given to him by Winter.

Pussy Cat came walking into the room a couple of hours later asking were was Winter and Wezzy. Gavin explained to her that they went to make a few errands and that they would be back soon. She went downstairs to fix her something to eat and noticed a note on the table from Weezy:

'Hey sis. I'm with Winter at the airport getting the tickets for us to leave tonight. Garvin's an angel! He gave us the money we need to be able to leave with Winter. I spoke with Stacks and he said he is waiting for us all. I'll see you shortly. Love Weezy'

After reading the note Pussy Cat got overly excited and went back upstairs to thank Garvin personally which turned into 45 minutes of steamy hot sex.

Once Wezzy and Winter got back they all chilled by the pool taking turns seducing Garvin until it was time to go catch their flight to Houston where Stacks had told them to go and wait with the rest of the girls.

Stacks arrived at the airport two hours after Winter and Wezzy and he was super tired when he got to the estate. Winter gave Stacks his ring to put on, which was a perfect fit. He then went to his private den to tally up his monthly earnings.

Shortly after unpacking, Winter went throughout the house passing out her gifts to the other girls while introducing Pussy Cat and Wezzy to the rest of the family.

CHAPTER 9

Back In Ohio

"Yo bleed. Check this out K. I was at a new pool spot "Vision 8" over on Cedar with Mackadoeshish kicking his ass on the table. We shooting the nine, then the baddest hoe I ever layed my pimpin' eyes on came strutting through the door looking to choose up on a pimp. I started to put that hoe under pimp arrest with all the reckless eyeballing she was doing.

"This hoe was so fine I wanted to take the hoe to Cleveland Clinic to get a sample of her DNA so that I could clone the bitch. That way I could see the bitch twice at one time. everybody in the pool hall was trying to spit game at the hoe. She shot em all down like a hunter do ducks during hunting season. Then all eyes was on me to see if I could knock the hoe.

"So you know me. I put a show on that I was gone make the bitch pay for in the end. I stepped to the bitch and said 'look hoe I'm going to do you a favor by giving you a chance to be with a real live pimp that's pimpin' at an all-time high but before I do that you gone have to pay me.' The bitch asked me why should she do that and give me all of her money? I told the hoe because she needs to 'get some order about her disorder and allow me to give her some instructions' that's gone save her 'from destruction because right now you are headed nowhere fast with yo renegade ass. Bitch break yourself of all your cash and get back on the stroll and go sell some ass.'

"That's when the hoe dug deep into her leather and sterling Lando bag and pulled out a bank roll she went to hand it to me then I told the hoe to put it on the table because I didn't know where her filthy hands been at. I picked the money up and counted it. The total was six thousand seven hundred and ten dollars. That's when I ice grilled the bitch and told the hoe that she was short three thousand two hundred and ninety dollars so go get the rest of my money."

"Guess what?" Stacks asked.

"What's that?" asked K.

"Right now as we speak that hoe on the track, with a jet pack on her back - getting my stacks." Stacks phone rang.

Stacks answered, "Money talk's bullshit walks what's it gone be?"

"Hey daddy, I got the rest of your money plus a little extra and I'm ready to come home wherever that may be," said Cherry.

"Well, I'll be there to get my money. But you need to work the track a couple of more hours that way you can make me some more money."

OG Stack$

"Stack daddy my feet hurt and I'm hungry. Can I just leave when you get here please."

"Naw bitch, you better walk real lightly and swallow your spit, turn some more tricks, and sucks some more dicks. Bitch you leave when the fuck I tell you to leave so just be looking out for a black Hummer. My driver will be there when its time. Until then, get money!"

Click! Stacks hung up the phone. Three hours later Stacks sent K and LA over to go pick up Cherry. He told them to look for a redbone with red hair who had a few freckles in her face. He explained to them that she was about 5' 2" in height and between 120 and 130 in weight. Her hair was down to her phat ass, she had two cherries tatted on her neck, and to top it all off she was bo legged to the bone.

"Dam. That bitch fine?" said K.

"Yeah she look like she good for about eight to ten thousand a week if she is put in the right places at the right time. When you bring the bitch back I'm going to fly to Houston so that I can set her up with her own website. Then get Jay the photographer to snap some hot shots of her. I'm going put her and this other hoe that Winter is bringing back named Pussycat on a video sucking and licking each other's pussy. I'm gonna run some copies and put them on the black market underground porn sites," said Stacks.

"Sounds good to me big hommie," replied K.

"Well go get that bitch so I can handle my business…"

CHAPTER 10

Pimp Choosin'

Stacks arrived in Houston hours later. He took a shower to freshen up, then headed down stairs for his mandatory meeting. He was carrying a bottle of Rose' as he stepped off the elevator that he added to his estate. He walked into his meeting room where his stable full of hoes awaited him. He was now 100 hundred hoes strong, when it came to his starting lineup.

He thought to himself how fortunate these hoes was to have a pimp ass nigga like himself running their lives for them. Once in the room Stacks noticed that, out of his ten starting bitches, there was one missing and this rubbed him the wrong way.

"Has anybody seen Carmella?" Stacks asked.

"She took a cab over to the Galleria early this morning for a date," said Summer.

"Ok, in today's meeting we will be welcoming our three new editions into the establishment."

Stacks handed all three girls a paper with his rules and regulations on it.

"What you ladies now hold in your hands are the rules and regulations that which you all shall live by as long as you are under my management. So read them, then read them again, then read them every morning that you wake up because there is no room for any misunderstandings unless you don't understand something that I wrote down on that paper. If that is the case speak now or forever hold your peace."

No one said anything.

"Ok, now with that out of the way, I would like to bring froth my second issue. Sin, you will be moving to Vegas with my cuzzin' on a business venture, so go pack your shit and be ready within the next two hours. And as for the rest of you girls you all will be a part of a video. Is there anything that anybody would like to discuss?"

Everybody remained silent.

"Ok. This meeting is a rap!" said Stacks.

After the meeting, Stacks sat by the pool enjoying the rest of the bottle of Rose' while watching his hoes play in the pool ass whole naked. Then his phone started ringing. He noticed that it was Carmella's number, so he answered it on the second ring.

"Bitch! Where the fuck you been at? You know that I have mandatory meetings whenever I touch down in the town."

A deep voice came through the other end of the phone.

"A pimpin! This is Pimpin' Crane out of Dallas. I'm known for pulling a pimp's hoe a.k.a Freeze. I was calling out of respect of the game to let you know I just touched a pimp's pocket and froze all your assets when comes to that hoe Carmella. I got that bitch under a new management so just keep it pimpin' pimpin'"

Click! The phone hug up. A couple of days later Stacks received another phone call from Pimpin' Crane saying the same thing about Summer and Peaches who was called earlier that day for a double date. Peaches took Summer instead of her sister because Cream, who was out on a date already.

Stacks started wondering who was this nigga that keep pulling his hoes because now he was not just touching a pimp's pocket, he was making major withdrawals out of them. So he called K up on the phone.

"Yo what up Bleed. I need you to send my second string of hoes."

"Stacks, you good?" K asked.

"Nah, them bitches Carmela, Summer and Peaches jumped ship on a pimp, so let LA know to get on the next thing smoking with Shay, Brooklyn and Megan. It's time for me to tighten up around this bitch," said Stacks.

"I got you Stacks. Later."

"Alright, later."

As soon as stacks hung up the phone Cream came walking into the kitchen where Stacks was fixing himself an energy drink.

"Daddy!" Cream said with the voice of someone who had lost their best friend.

"What's up lil mama, what's on your mind?"

"Well Stacks, I was thinking about my sister."

"There is nothing to think about. She chose up on another pimp's pimpin," replied Stacks.

"I don't believe that my sister would do that without telling me to do the same thing. Just last week we was talking about how good you are to us."

"Well this week, as you can see, the bitch changed her mood like a DJ change songs at the club."

"Stacks me and my sister are close and deep down in my head I know something is wrong and I'm gone find out one way or the other."

"Do what you gotta do, just don't let whatever you do interrupt you getting money cause just like your sister you can be out like the old set. We can replace you with the new."

Cream regarded Stacks with a puzzle look on her face.

"What the fuck are you staring at?" Stacks asked harshly. "Get the fuck outta my face."

Cream was on the edge of saying something but instead fell in place and followed suit like the hoe she was and did what she was told to do.

Ten hours later, LA was pulling up in a cab from the airport with two pink-toes and one ride or die bitch from Brooklyn, by the name of "Brooklyn." Shay and Magan were the two pink toes out of Akron, Ohio who were the baddest street walkers the track ever scene.

Shay was about 5' 2" with jet black hair, slanted eyes and high cheek bones. When Stacks first met her, it was in the parking lot of Lisa's Cabinet, a strip club in Akron. She had this trick ass white man with the name Norman on his license plates squirming like a fish out of water, from the head job she was getting him. As Stacks was getting into his ride, Shay was exiting the car looking like the white trash she was. She looked at Stacks and said "Hey daddy! Why don't you let me show you how I got the name vacuum head Shay. I guarantee you, that I suck a dick so well, I can suck a nail outta board, before you get a chance to pull it out with a hammer."

Stacks told the hoe, "Being that you a dope fiend ass bitch, Imma give you a hoe pass to get yourself together for this pimpin' now get yo dusty ass in the car before I change my mind." Shay jumped in and Stacks dropped the bitch of at the Detox Center and picked her back up five days later. He put her in a hotel for 30 days straight, left the bitch with no clothes or shoes, just a bag full of condoms with a gang of soap and razors to shave her pussy.

He would have LA take the bitch food three times a day and he directed all late night and early morning traffic in her direction. After 30 days of her being drug free and selling pussy on the upscale level, Stacks put the bitch to work at the Vanity Wash.

As for Megan she was Shay's cuzzin' who used to be in an abusive relationship. She came to Stacks begging for a job at the Vanity Wash. She had been married straight out of high school at the age of eighteen to the guy who took her virginity. She was married to him for ten years and had never been with another man besides him. So Stacks put the bitch to work and she became one of the favorites amongst the neighborhood hustlers. She was 5' 9" with big titties and blond hair and her tongue was pierced.

She had a wide fat ass and kinda looked like Amber Rose with hair. Then there was Brooklyn a.k.a Passion who was eye candy to any man's eyes. She was so beautiful with her hair in extensions braided to the back, her skin reminded you of a hot coco drink with hazel eyes. Her lips were full and thick and her breast was a mouth full - not too big and not too small. But her ass looked like two bowling balls stuffed in a pair of jeans. She

OG Stack$

was Stacks' head bitch that grew up in the grimy streets of Red Hook, section in Brooklyn, New York.

The way she carried herself made her stand out like a Christian priest at a Islamic gathering on Friday during their holiest month. She was a seasoned bitch who sold pussy to some of the most famous guys the entertainment business.

"What up doe Stacks?" said "LA."

"Yo! I'm good just a little on edge not knowing what's going through these hoes head taking off on a pimp and fucking with these plastic ass pimps. I checked with one of my pimp pals and asked him did he know this nigga named Crane or Freeze. Come to find out they say he been pulling a lot of pimp's hoes all around town. Most of their main bitches but don't nobody know this nigga for real cause there is not one pimp or hoe that has ever seen this lame."

"So what you are telling me is that you lost three of your top notch hoes to some Casper the pimpin' ghost ass nigga," said LA.

"Yeah, that is the crazy part about it. What I need you to do is from now on drop off and pick up my hoes for all local dates."

"I got you stacks. Don't worry. I am going to hit the streets on a late night and blend in to find out who this nigga is. Also, I am going to send for a few of my soldiers so they can be on call. This shit get crazy," replied LA.

"Okay you do that. In the mean time I have the go chop it up with Moses. You should remember him. He was in Leavenworth with us," said Stacks.

"Oh yeah, I remember that Mexican Mafia muthafucka. You dealing with that snake?"

"Yeah, I know he's a snake but he has this private jet that I am going to buy off of him so I can get a round quicker and be the jetsetter I need to be. He has an elegant Italian piaggo Avanti."

"Like I would know what the fuck that is. I didn't start flying until I went to the Fed's," said LA.

"Well, LA' it's worth it because I am tired of waiting in line to fly out of town. That shit gets old so I gotta step my game up. That is probably why the hoes left because I have gotten too complacent with what I got. I need to get more of everything!" said Stacks.

"Yeah, big homey, if you say so. But for right now I am about to watch the game. Lebron is playing tonight."

"Okay," said Stacks.

"Later," replied LA.

OG Stack$

In the meantime, Stacks contemplated how he would save his empire from being systematically dismantled by some invisible pimp.

Stacks was one of the most successful pimps in the game in the country. He had no plans of letting that title go. No matter what, he was going to get people know that he was still pimpin' in the game!

Chapter 11

Black Murda

Carmela was struggling to get out of the grip that Crane had on her in the basement of the house she was now being held hostage in. She tried to make her way up the stairs that led out of the house to get back before Stacks had his meeting he usually had whenever he returned home from out of town.

She was pleading with Crane asking could she leave because her pimp would be looking for her. Crane grabbed her by the arm pushed her up against the wall and pinned her. Then said to her "I'm not allowing you to go nowhere bitch."

"Please let me go you are hurting me," cried Carmella.

"I tell you what if you suck my dick then I might think about letting you go."

"Look, you sorry bastard, I've told you for the 100th time that my lip service is not for free or cheap. I'm a bonified hoe you fucking maggot!" said Carmella.

Crane grabbed her by her hair and threw her to the floor face first then he straddled her from the back holding her hair while he was banging her head on the floor saying "Bitch I told you to fuck with a real pimp!"

Carmella was crying telling Crane to leave her alone in between sobs, screaming for help.

"Bitch! Can't nobody hear you down here. You better get some act right up in this muthafucka or you gonna die tonight hoe."

Crane begin unbuttoning her jeans while again saying "You gone fuck with a pimp and sell some pussy for me bitch!" He began to put his hands inside of her jeans trying to shove his fingers into her pussy.

All of a sudden the basement door opened up. Then entered the frame of a 6' 4" 270 pound guy named "Black Murda." Black Murda, started descending down the stairs.

"Nigga! Didn't I tell you not to fuck with that hoe. We don't rape bitches. We sell hoes. Now get up off of her and grab these needles because its more than one way to skin a cat."

Crane got up off of her then grabbed the needles from Black Murda, while Black Murda helped Carmella up. Then said to her "Look bitch don't take this shit personal because it's strictly about business for me," then he punched the bitch so hard that he knocked yesterday's cum up out of her mouth and knocked her out all at the same time.

"Alright now, hand me them needles. I got some of the best raw uncut heroin money can buy up in these needles." Black Murda begin tying a belt around her arm looking for a vein. As soon as he found one, he injected her with a nice amount of the drug.

"Now if this don't kill the bitch by the time she wake up she gone be so high that she's not going to know what's going on, let alone stops us from making money off of her mutha fucking ass. She will be making money for us hand over fist," said Black-Murder.

"Man Black! Let me fuck this hoe one good time. That's all I need," asked Crane.

"Naw mutha-fucka. What you want to fuck this cum bucket for? Plus I'm taking the bitch to the warehouse with the rest of them bitches. Oh yeah, did you make that call to her pimp and tell that nigga what I said for you to say? That way he won't be out looking for this bitch."

"Yeah! I called that nigga and said exactly what you told me to say. Also I noticed that she got a lot of other hoes numbers on her phone. We should call some more and set up a date for two, that way we can get two at one time."

"Don't worry about that right now because in due time we will have the opportunity to snatch up every street walker there is in this town."

Then they took Carmela to the warehouse, put her into the built-in room section of the warehouse and for the next day or so they had her flat back totally unaware of her surroundings or dealings. Then a day later Crane called two chicks out of Carmela's cell phone, set up a double date, then snatched two more of Stacks hoes. He shot em up wit "dogg-food," another name for heroin, and took them to the warehouse, as well.

By now Crane and his big homie, Black Murda, had the warehouse up and fully running with an A-list of underground clients. They had a total of 12 prostitutes that they had kidnapped from different hoe strolls all throughout Houston, selling pussy and sucking dicks, while under the influence of dogg-food.

By the fifth day of operation shit got crazy! The prostitutes were getting immune to the drug, so it took more doses to keep them high and Crane gave Peaches too much of the drug and she died from an overdose.

Once Black Murda found out about what went down he gave Crane strict orders not to touch none of the prostitutes anymore and for him to go dump the dead body off in an alley over by the hoe-stroll, to make it look like another drug addicted prostitute had died of an overdose of heroin. Crane loaded the dead body into the trunk of his car, drove to Houston, pulled up on Telephone Road, right by the Mustang Hotel in between the alley and Projects and unloaded the body.

Crane did not notice the black SUV that was sitting off in the cut, where LA was watching as he unloaded the familiar face of a female that appeared to be dead, or just unconscious. Either way he was determined to find out. So as Crane was preparing to get back into his car to leave, LA had already snuck up behind Crane and hit him over the head and knocked him out.

He went over to the body, reached down to see if Peaches was breathing by putting his finger under her nose. Then checked her neck for a pulse. He realized that the female he finally identified as Peaches was dead. So he picked Crane up, took him to the back of the truck and hog-tied him with duct tape, covering his mouth. He secured Crane in the truck and pulled off calling Stacks and informing him to meet him in the guest house.

Back at the estate. LA arrived driving all the way to the guest house. He pulled up to the front door and he jumped out, grabbed Crane up, and then took him in the house. He dropped him on the floor like a sack of potatoes. Crane instantly woke up from the fall.

By LA being good with his hands, he loved to fight, so this was a great opportunity to put his hands on a muthafucka and catch some wreak. So he cut the duct tape off of Crane, then said, "How did Peaches die? And where are the other two hoes at?!"

"Fuck you bitch ass nigga, I don't owe you an explanation," replied Crane.

"That's too bad young nigga," said LA. Then LA slung a flurry of blows, catching Crane to the jaw and head. Crane rushed LA almost knocking him down. LA stumbled back regaining his balance. Then LA kneed Crane in the stomach and hit him to the body with two hard blows that knocked the wind out of Crane. Stacks came walking in as LA was banging Crane's head into the wall, asking him over and over again about Peaches dead body and for the where abouts of Carmela and Summer.

"Yo LA! What the fuck is going on up in this bitch? This ain't no damn UFC arena and who the fuck is that nigga anyway?!" yelled Stacks.

"This bitch ass nigga was dumping Peaches dead body in the alley over by the track where yo hoes be killing cash at," replied LA.

"Oh yeah, look out man, let me holla at this nigga... What up you fucking maggot, how did my hoe come up dead? You had something to do with that?" asked Stacks.

"Fuck you too, what make you think Imma tell you something when I didn't tell that nigga nothing?" replied Crane.

"Oh, bitch ass nigga, you gone talk."

Then Stacks grabbed his 9 mm out of his holster he had on. Then pointed the gun at Crane's left foot and shot him. Then as Crane fell to the ground screaming and shouting, Stacks pointed the gun to Crane's head and said: "You know what bitch ass nigga? Hoes come a dime a dozen so to be truthful, fuck them bitches and you too."

Then Stacks went to blow his head off but Crane shouted, "Ok Ok! I'll talk, please! Just don't shoot me!"

Crane then gave up all the information about Murda and his plan to keep kidnapping street prostitutes and shoot em up wit the dogg-food. That way they won't know what's going on or who they are. He then gave Stacks the street address to the warehouse, in return for his life.

But instead Stacks turned to LA and said, "Kill that piece of shit."

LA shot him in the back of his head execution style. Stacks gave specific orders for LA to go to the warehouse and kill everybody in that bitch without a slit and a clit and to bring all the pussy back to the estate.

He was going to get Tina to nourish them all back to health, so he could put em down. After that, Stacks went to break the news to Cream about her sister being dead.

When he told her she became hysterical, screaming, crying and throwing stuff that was expensive. So Stacks smacked sense back into her head. Then told her to go somewhere and collect herself, because those who were responsible for her sister's death was going to "pay for it.... with their life!"

Chapter 12

"Sin"

"Oh shit, this dick feel so good," said Tequila to her F.B.I. agent friend she had been seeing for quite some time now. She knew him back when she was ten years younger, during her years as a Private, in the armed forces. At that time he was a Lieutenant.

Now he's an F.B.I. agent. She crossed his path at the airport on her way back home from a wild, but prosperous, weekend in Italy. He questioned her about her life, so she explained to him that she was working as a professional call girl. He told her that he was working for the government and that he wanted to spend time with her, as long as she could keep a secret.

"Gimme that dick Shawn."

He showed her no mercy as he pounded in and out of her wet pussy. He let loose a low long moan as he began to go deeper into her. He was cumming as she was digging her nails into his back. Then he brought her to climax. Her body went into spasms that shot through every inch of her body.

"Mmmm, that felt so good," Shawn said, as he fell over onto his back, breathing extra hard. " 'T' baby, I feel so good every time I am with you. I just wish things could be different between us."

"Shawn you know it has to be this way. It's better for both of us. Not that I don't enjoy being with you. I just enjoy not being tied down, as well as what I do even better. I was the Warden of Leavenworth Penitentiary for five years after I got out the Army. Now that I do what I do, I only wish I would have started years ago," said Tequila with regret.

"Yeah, I guess you're right. Because with my job schedule I really can't enjoy a real relationship for real," replied Shawn.

At almost the exact same time they both got up out of bed, Tequila went into the bathroom while Shawn picked up the numerous amount of condoms that had been scattered on the floor from his all night sex-capade with Tequila. Once Tequila was done in the bathroom she came out explaining to Shawn why she couldn't wait for them to leave together.

Ever since Peaches' death there was a driver that picked her up and dropped her off on her dates. She told Shawn goodbye. When she got into the car, her cell phone started buzzing,

"Hello?" said Tequila.

"Yo Tequila!" said Stacks.

"What's up daddy?" she asked.

"LA is taking you to the airport, so you can go meet up with a client in England," he explained.

"Daddy I'm tired and I wanna come home," she said with exhaustion.

"Your flight is a 14 hour ride, so get some rest on the plane. I put you in first class and Cherri packed your bags, for a two week trip. The money you made; put it in the envelope under the seat, then call me as soon as you touch down."

"Yes! Stacks, I'll call you as soon as I get there." Then the phone hung up.

"Yesssss!" moaned Precious as Sin was sticking her tongue in and out of Precious' ass. Her sexual moans were arousing Sin, which made her do things with her tongue that Precious had never thought could be done.

"Mmmm, your ass taste so good," said Sin, coming up for air only long enough to sink her head into Precious' rain forest that was dripping wet. Precious' pussy lips were like two swollen lips. Her eyes were closed enjoying every lick and succulent suck of Sin's mouth. As her toes curled up she grabbed the back of Sin's head pulling it closer to her, begging her to keep going. She then began to shiver and shake.

"Oooh Sin I'm cumming... Ohhh shit baby! I'm cumming.. Ohhh God, Sin please suck it! Suck this pussy baby!"

Then Precious layed there for a hot second, got up and strapped on the twelve inch, thick dildo that vibrated and turned Sin around into the doggy style position. Reaching over to grab the extra virgin olive oil, Precious poured some in her hands then started stroking the dildo as if it was her very own. The sight of the thick over-sized dildo had Sin in awe, mentally preparing herself for what was about to take place.

Precious had gotten Sin so drunk on Patron and had given her some Triple Stacks ecstasy pills, then told her that tonight she was going to lose her virginity all over again, in the aspect of taking it up the ass.

So now Precious stood behind her stroking this monstrous dildo. She then poured the olive oil onto Sin's ass, letting it go in between the crack, reaching her asshole. Precious took her thumb and slid it into Sin's ass while her fingers were on her back. It was as if Sin's ass was a bowling ball. She started moving her thumb in a circular motion. Sin was wiggling and jiggling her ass because it was a new feeling.

She was loving the fact that Precious had her thumb inside of her. But now she wanted something bigger! The triple stacks had her ready. Then Precious eased the tip of the thick dildo into Sin's ass, as Sin let out a long loud grunt, followed by a sexy moan. This turned Precious on to the point where she gripped Sin by the hips and pushed a few more inches into her tight Asian ass.

"Ooooh Precious! Yes! Sooo good, it hurts! Ahhhh! Shit easy please!!" Sin cried.

Then Precious turned on the dildo so that it could vibrate as she slowly fucked Sin in the ass.

"Oooh SHIT! Goddamn! Ohhhh! God please I can't take it!" Sin screamed.

Precious was so turned on she didn't realize the long, deep, hard strokes had Sin crying in pain from the pleasure of the thrusting dick. Precious reached around, then started massaging Sin's nipples. Sin panted, breathing heavy as Precious yelled, "Whose yo mamma? Tell me bitch! Whose yo mamma?!"

Sin could not respond as Precious had bust her ass wide open going all the way up in her. Sin began to beg her to stop. The pain had become excruciating.

"Shut up you little bitch I'll stop when I'm ready!" yelled Precious as she spanked Sin's ass. She then reached down and started playing with Sin's clitoris, bringing Sin to orgasm that continued on until Precious pulled out then buried herself in between Sin's ass cheeks, eating her pussy from the back, turning her orgasms into a five minute release of cum.

Then Sin collapsed onto her stomach still pulsating and shivering. Sin thought to herself that it must run in her blood, because like Stacks had made her feel feelings while fucking that no other man made her feel; the same way Precious had made her cum like no other woman.

She has had plenty of lesbian sex, but none like the way she did tonight and she planned to do whatever was needed to be done to have Precious to herself, without K in the picture. Her mind started to wander, how could she get rid of K, without Precious knowing it was all her doing?

Shay and Megan took turns as they both sucked on K's 13 inch dick. He had them flown in for the weekend since Precious and Sin stayed at it every night. K couldn't get no pussy from Precious since Sin had come to Las Vegas a few weeks ago. Stacks gave K a two for one deal since K was his man, but he still separated his pimpin' from his friendship.

Shay's hot horny ass couldn't wait to have K feel her up. She had never in her life seen a dick as big as K's. All her life she had looked for a King Kong dick to abuse her pink pussy. It was the reason that she became the hoe she was. It wasn't for the money or the drugs she no longer used. It was the hunt for a chocolate tootsie roll that she now had in front of her eyes.

As for Megan, she was used to an oversized dick because she had privately been getting her pussy and ass tore out the frame by Stacks on the late night, ever since she gave him that suit case full of money that she had won at the Casino in Kansas, Missouri when she was out on a date.

Stacks had cut her off due to the fact that he said he was tricking off his dick. So this was something she missed, a big dick. Now she only hoped that K could dick her down good like Stacks. They both was licking the sides of K's dick, while he was playing in their pussies. Then Shay pushed Megan away as she slowly straddled K, easing his dick up in her pussy. She slid down the dick like a stripper slide down a pole, as Megan sat on his face. Shay was moving in her own rhythm up and down on his dick, picking up the pace. She was immune to the pain because she was abused and beaten as a child by her step mother, so she could take the pain.

K sucked away as Megan rode his face, then Megan did a 180 on his face, now facing Shay as they both began sucking on each other's lips and tongues. This went on for about 20 minutes. Then Megan and Shay switched positions for another 20 minutes. K put Shay in the doggy style position and was fucking her while she sucked her cousin's pussy, swallowing her juices for about 30 minutes. Then they switched up and this went on until everyone exploded. K layed in between the two women until the next morning when his phone started ringing.

"Hello? Who is this?" he questioned.

"What you mean who is this? Nigga where the fuck is you at? And why weren't you at the club last night?!" demanded Precious.

"I'm out of town taking care of some business for your cousin. I'll be back tonight or in the morning. I didn't think you'd even notice I was gone. Especially since you got your chick on the side," said K.

"Do I detect a lil' bit of jealousy in your voice?" said Precious. "Look Precious, I gotta get ready so I'll call you later on when I'm finished doing what I'm doing. I'll talk to you later," he said.

"Ok baby, bye!"

All the while she had been on the phone, Sin layed there, pretending to be asleep. As soon as she hung up Sin turned her over, raised her up and began to kiss Precious on the neck.

"Hmmm, good morning my little China doll," Precious said.

"Good morning baby, what's on the agenda for the day? Do I get to have you all to myself without worries of life?" asked Sin.

"Yes sweetie, come on let's take a nice hot shower and go out to breakfast, before I take you shopping."

"Oh that sounds lovely. Come on baby," said Sin sweetly.

They both took a shower together, soaping each other up and then left for breakfast at the Golden Coral before they went shopping.

Chapter 13

Off Paper!

Today was October 8th, a full year had went and past and today Stacks had received his papers from his probation officer telling him that his probation was now being terminated. Stacks was making plans for a night of celebration. So he called up his pimp associate, Sergio, who was a certified pimp out of Oklahoma. He owned some land in Dallas, Texas the size of two football fields with a private landing strip for personal jets.

Most of his money came from being connected to the Mexican Drug Cartel. Pimpin' Sergio had appeared on the front cover of the Billionaire's Edition of Forbes Magazine. He had the biggest telecommunication and Software Company in Mexico. His headquarters was in Mexico City.

The phone rang three times before Sergio picked up.

"Buenos dias, que pasa!" said Sergio.

"Buenos dias amigo! How you doin' my friend?" asked Stacks.

"Stacks! Vato coco! What's up with you? It's been a long time since I have heard from you. An associate of mine was visiting a few months back and had mentioned to me that he sold his parent's jet to some black guy, by the name of Stacks. When he said your name I asked him 'was this guy named 'Stacks,' the hustler out of Brooklyn, NY?' He said 'that's the Stacks!,' he knew was a big time pimp from Cleveland. It wasn't until he described you to me that I knew it had to be you. So how is my friend?" said Sergio.

"Yo! Sergio! I've come a long way from the small time mule I used to be. It's been a total of six years since the last time our paths crossed," replied Stacks.

"Well what is it that I can do for you vato?" asked Sergio.

"I am celebrating my release from prison a year ago today. I am officially off papers and would like to have a party at your mansion and call it the 'Player's Ball.' That's when a bunch of pimps and hoes get together and crown the pimp of the year and I know I can win that crown hands down!" explained Stacks.

"When are you planning on having this 'Players Ball' as you call it?" asked Sergio.

"What about three weeks from now? That'll give me time to promote this event on a major level."

"I don't see any problem with that. Anything for a friend. I am going to invite a few of my associates and fly in some of my bitches from Juarez, Mexico," said Sergio.

"Cool wit me pimpin. So make it for October 22nd!"

"Ok the 22nd it is! Adios amigo!" replied Sergio.

"Adios!"

"Yo Pussy Cat! I need to see you in my office," Stacks said over the intercom in the room where Pussy Cat was laying down watching TV. Stacks had video and intercom systems installed in every room of the house. So the "Eagle" was watching at all times, as he would often say.

It also allowed him to burn DVDs of the girls' freak shows they would have whenever it was two or more of them together drinking. He had a 24 hour website, where you could visit at any time to enjoy the company of a female or how many of them were in the basement. He had the girls on a schedule where they would take turns being on the camera in the basement.

Knock, knock!

"Come in!" Stacks said.

"Hey daddy, you want some of this Pussy Cat?" asked Pussy Cat.

"Now that's not what I called you in here for. What I need you to do is grab this pen and paper and write down what I tell you."

"Ok Stacks," Pussy Cat replied.

"I need 100,000 flyers, 50,000 posters, and about 20,000 copies of Weezy's birthday party. Make 300 tickets and 100 VIP tickets. We're going to sell the regular tickets at $2,000 a piece and the VIP tickets at $3,000. Anybody that pays at the entrance pays $2,500." Stacks explained.

"Put 'Pimp King Stacks Players Ball' on the tickets, with a group picture with all of you on it. The picture I had ya'll take in Vegas last month at the 'Doll House.' That way mufuckas can see I'm 50 hoes strong. Between everybody here, the girls at the Doll House, the girls at both strip clubs, and the girls from the Vanity Wash," he dictated.

"Set up a meetin' at the local radio stations as well as a few out of town and with B.E.T., HBO, Showtime, and the Oxygen channels. Also run an invite commercial on YouTube, then get in touch with my man from Harlem, Steve at 'Party All Da Time Entertainment.' And then let me know the details I just gave you," he said.

"Tell all the girls I said to be ready in the morning. We're flying to New York to go shopping for my event. That'll be all for now Pussy Cat."

"You sure you don't need anything else daddy?" she asked.

"Nah bitch, get yo thirsty ass outta here and go do what the fuck I just said," Stacks ordered.

"Alright daddy, let me know if you change your mind."

The next morning everybody was dressed and ready to go. The whole entourage was in place, from the drivers to the body guards, along with all of Stacks stable full of hoes. Stacks gave specific orders not to bring nothing except the clothes on they backs. He was feeling extra good, so everybody was getting all new everything, all the way down to the driver, LA, and his crew of silver back gorillas.

They arrived in New York then went straight to the Waldorf Astoria Hotel; a Five Star Hotel where he had reserved the Presidential Penthouse Suite and the whole floor underneath. He brought three Gucci outfits with him that had a million dollars in each one. "Party All Da Time Entertainment" had set up an interview with a few radio stations to promote the big event.

For the first few days he handled business first. Then he went to his old hood on Atlantic and hung out with a few cats he knew from way back when. The next day he went to Soho to get him a few tailored made suits and a few pairs of "gators." The girls went to Sax's Fifth Avenue and spent out of control, buying all the exclusive outfits, handbags, heels and undergarments. Everybody met up on Broadway to buy their minks and furs.

Then in the Diamond District Stacks spent over a million dollars on jewels for himself and the girls. He even bought his homeboy LA and his crew minks and presidential Rolexes.

Stacks bought a full length spotted Chinchilla with a matching brim. Then everybody headed to the hotel.

Brooklyn asked Stacks if she could go visit her mom. So he let her go that night but he told her that they would be leaving first thing in the morning.

That night Stacks surprised everybody with back stage passes to the Jay-Z concert. He was performing at the Barclays Center. Everybody got dressed and Stacks appeared at the show with his hoes. Then after the show, he had his hoes pass out the flyers to his Player's Ball. It seemed like every artist that was from Brooklyn was back stage poppin' bottles and blazin' trees.

Then he saw her, he thought his eyes was playin' tricks on him. There she stood - Isis. He at one point in time felt it was a blessing from God to be able to visualize her beauty. But now as she stood there, all he could think about was him catching the TD Syndrome, if he didn't keep it pimpin. So he popped his collar, then blew right past her like a breeze on a hot summer day. Which reaffirmed all over again that pimpin' was for the strong minded and tough dick mufuckas. It took a lot out of him to keep it pimpin' and straight pass one of the baddest females on the planet.

After the "After Party," Stacks went back to his suite. On the way up in the elevator Stacks invited Cherri to spend the evening with him. She had never had the opportunity to get beat down by Stacks' "Iron Rod." He felt like it was finally her turn. Especially since it had been months since her acceptance into his stable. Not to mention all the money that she had made him. She had been begging for him - for this moment for quite some time now.

As he pumped unlimited dick all up inside her guts, she felt happier than a fat bitch losing weight on Jenny Craig, still bein' able to enjoy all her favorite foods. Stacks put it down on Cherri all night, until the sun came up. Right before it was time to go, he took a shower. He called Tequila on the hotel phone and told her to gather everybody and meet him downstairs in the lobby. Then he called LA, who had some Jamaican chick he met the night before at the show. He told them to pack up and that it was time to go. On the way to the airport, Stacks got a call from his man K.

"Yo Stacks, what up wit you? Are you still in New York?" K asked.

"Yeah, headed to the jet as we speak. What's on your mind?" asked Stacks.

"I need you to add Nonchalant to your roster of entertainment. So he can perform at your event," said K.

"K, my man is you serious? This ain't no amateur night at the Apollo! It's going to be a lot of big time playas on the house that day. Do you really think that sun can rise to the occasion?" replied Stacks.

"No doubt! He can hold his own. I wouldn't ask you to do this if I wasn't sure that he can get it poppin' in that bitch. I heard him perform before. He set it off at Cobo Hall in Detroit for that ballin' ass nigga Skeet. Ask yo mans LA. He was the gun man on duty that night," explained K.

"Alright K, you know I'm on some pimp' or die shit, so he can't be poppin' no weak lyrics," said Stacks.

"Nah bleed on some real live pimp shit, his style is like 'God Bless Da Dead' *(Pimp C.)*. But his deliverance is laid back like Fabulous," described K.

"Alright tell his manager that I'll let him perform as long as he let me get a video producer to shoot a video of his performance. Have his manager get in touch with Jennifer," said Stacks, "that way she can write up a contract. It'll be his song but my video, otherwise just dead the whole thing."

"Yo bleed you never cease to amaze me! One way or the other you gonna shake the money tree. But I ain't mad at ya! Aye, pimpin' ain't easy, it's all about the Benjamins, them dead Presidents," laughed K.

"Speaking of loot, do you have my take for this month's earnings off the club? And when you gone kick my ten percent in the ass off that hot mill I gave you?" asked Stacks.

"I got you when I come to the ball, I'll bring this month's take. As for the Mill ticket, Imma get at you in the near future," replied K.

"Oh yeah! Them hoes Shay and Megan had diarrhea of the mouth when they got back in town from fucking with you. They was explaining to me about the situation with Precious carrying you like a Muslim during Ramadan! Leaving you hungry for that muffin. Word is, the lil' Asian dried up your well and got that pussy on lock. How you let that go down?" asked Stacks.

"Yeah! Sin must got that ill nah-nah, because I barely see your cousin. Then when I do that lil' bitch Sin be all in the mix. I ain't trippin, she can have her fun and Imma have mines on the side. Once she get it all out her system, she'll be back on my dick!" K said. "Right now she like a kid with a new toy, it'll wear off."

"Well my nigga, I'll get at you," said Stacks.

"Alright big bro. Later."

As they hung up Stacks began to board the private jet. He was exhausted. So he kicked his feet up, had Winter remove his shoes, and dozed off to a foot massage. A few hours later Stacks felt the plane wheels touch the ground and woke up. His phone was buzzing. It was a text from Jennifer telling him that she was at the Estate in his office waiting on him, so she could go over the bank statements, and a few other very important business matters.

Once back at the Estate, Stacks poured himself a drink then sat down behind his imported mahogany desk.

"So Jennifer, tell me how is my business doing?" he asked.

"Well Stacks everything is running well, except for the Doll House. Tina shut it down and put it under quarantine. One of the girls had Staff and it spread to one of the clients. Now his lawyer is trying to sue. Evidentially the guy was married and went home and his wife is now hospitalized. She already had some type of skin disease and this Staff infection broke her out even worse," she explained.

"So right now that's what is going on. The Vanity Wash had a shootout in the parking lot. There were no casualties. But business has slowed down. Your friend Mr. Turner in Leavenworth, called me the other day. He says he is grateful for the monthly deposits you have been sending him and he told me to ask you if you can pay for his daughter's graduation and prom arrangements. I was also thinking that with all the money in the oversea account, you should open a few more accounts and invest in some land in India," she suggested.

"Within the next five to ten years India will be one of the richest countries on earth. I have an investor over there ready to invest in the medical field. Right now in America all the top surgeons and doctors that are coming out of college are from India. Now is the time to invest."

Jennifer continued, "Plus in the underground world, prostitution is at an all-time high. They're breeding girls strictly for it. I figure we can build a Doll House over there and as soon as the girls get legal we can pay the parents anywhere from five to ten thousand American dollars and place the girls in the Doll House to work or swap out an American girl."

"I see somebody's been doing their homework. First thing first, send ten stacks to my man's Poppa Locka's daughter's mother for her graduation and prom. Buy her a little cheap ass car. A Toyota Camry, but make sure it's brand new. Now how much money are we talking about that's in the bank?" he asked.

"A little over a hundred million," she replied.

"Ok, Imma call my banker and have him transfer 5 million to the investor, for the medical investment. Then I want you to get on a plane personally and take that hoe Cream with you. She need to get away for a minute. She still fucked up over Peaches' death," said Stacks.

"As for moving some of that money to another account, that won't be necessary. I have a new foreign account in another country, I'll handle that at a later date," said Stacks.

"Well I guess that concludes the business. Now what else needs to be addressed?" he asked.

Then Jennifer stood up, walked to the door, locked it and turned around, taking her glasses off as she let her hair down.

She walked over to where Stacks was sitting and started unbuttoning her blouse and slowly took it off. Then she began to slip out of her pencil thin skirt. She stood before him in her pink Victoria's Secret panties and bra.

"Look big daddy" she said as she pulled out her titties. She started kissing and licking them, then moved her hips as if she was listening to a slow song of her own. She then got on her knees and unzipped his pants and pulled out his dick, held it in her hand, and started smacking her face with it. Stacks looked down and started thinking to himself that Christina Aguilera had to have a twin, because Jennifer was a spitting image of her. Stack's dick grew in her hand. She then put his huge head into her mouth, slowly sucking his dick as he gently rubbed her hair.

"You like this big black dick?" he asked.

"Yes daddy, oooh yes!" Jennifer exclaimed in between sucks, as she would gag from him pushing her head down on his oversized throbbing cock. Stacks grabbed her breast as he sat up letting his pants fall down over his knees. Jennifer, with her other hand pulled them all the way off. She continued to suck on his dick, like it was a delicacy. Stacks was now standing straight up, like his member - at full attention.

"Suck this dick bitch," Stacks ordered.

"Please talk dirty to me daddy, don't hold back!"

"Shut up bitch! And suck my dick!"

"Yes baby!" Jennifer replied. Then he shoved his dick back into her mouth.

"Suck it harder, you nasty white bitch!" he yelled.

Then Stacks reached into his desk drawer and grabbed a magnum condom and handed it to Jennifer. She opened it and put it on her mouth and sucked it on to his penis. He then laid her on her back, spread her legs wide open, as he slowly slid himself into her tight pussy. Felt like a tight fitted pair of leather gloves going on over and over again. Stacks pushed harder as Jennifer gasped and grunted then started to squirm.

"Oooh Stacks that dick feels so good! Push deeper daddy! Oooh yes give it all to me!" she yelled.

Stacks started with a slow rhythm, then started increasing the momentum as her pussy loosened up. He kept pushing deeper until he was all the way up in her. She had turned blood shot red.

"Oooh shit that dick is feeling so good!!"

He started grinding up in her.

"Harder, harder! Oh please fuck me harder!" He then took both her legs, raised them up and put them on his shoulder, reached around and gripped her ass. Then started banging away. She was screaming and the more she screamed the harder

Stacks would fuck her. He fantasized about fucking Isis; he picked up speed.

"I'm cumming! Oooh shit Stacks I'm cumming! Yes! Yes! Oh God yes, thank you god- oh god!" she yelled.

Then as he was about to cum, he pulled out, snatched the condom off, and bust his load all in her face and said, "How is that for a black man?" Then she sucked him dry.

Stacks was off paper and he was ridin' high! He felt on top of the world. He had stacked plenty of green and had it hid all over the world. At times he felt untouchable!

Now it was time to really live it up and celebrate! But Stacks always knew in the back of his mind, to ALWAYS be on the lookout. That was the only way to be to stay pimpin' in this game...

About the Author

Yasin abdul-mujib was born and raised as a Muslim all his young life. He studied at a prestigious all male Islamic School in Dewsbury Yorkshire England at the age of 11. He knew nothing of the street lifestyle until the divorce of his parents at age 14.

Subsequently, he experienced what it is to live the life of a non-sheltered child when he went to a juvenile detention home months after the divorce. This led him to living the life of crime, finding himself in and out of state and federal institutions.

Living the life of two worlds: one as a Muslim and another as a heartless criminal, he had the best of both worlds. It wasn't until his last "bit" that he started using his skills as a writer. He wrote a book, then more came to follow. Now as a writer and author he lives the life of a true "OG" to the game of life, reaping the benefits from the fruits of his labor.

Pimpasaurus

1. **Beat your feet** – Get to walking and go sell some pussy.
2. **Bonafied** – A thoroughbred Hoe.
3. **Burnt Chicken** – A hoe that's no good.
4. **Footballin** – Faking or Playing games.
5. **Fresh Meat** – A turn out or a new how that's green.
6. **Glue** – A hoe that has that, come back pussy that leaves a mufucka stuck on stupid.
7. **Hoe Down** – Get down with a pimp.
8. **Hoe pass** – when a hoe is excused for some dumb shit but pays for it in the long run.
9. **Lame** – A no-body or nothing.
10. **Killing Cash**- Making money hand over first.
11. **Maggot**- A low life pimp that's simpin.
12. **Main Line**- A pimps bottom bitch.
13. **Pimpadee-Mack-Pimp-Playa**- A nigga pimpin, mackin and playin' a Dolly Pardon out of her money.
14. **Pimpalicious** – Good enough to pimp.
15. **Pink Toe**—A White hoe or a snow bunny.
16. **Promoter** –Pimp.
17. **Reckless Eye Ballin** – Checking out another Pimp.
18. **Seasoned** – Up on game or been in the game with different Pimp.
19. **Simp** – Fake pimp in the game.
20. **Smut** – A nasty hoe.
21. **TD Syndrome** – Tender Dick.

22. **Tender Dick** – Fake ass Pimp; A Simp; Soft hearted.
23. **The Eyes** – When a person is embarrassed.
24. **The Stroll** – A street where hoes turn tricks.
25. **Trick** – A date spending money on sex.
26. **Tricking** – To buy sex.
27. **Turn Out** – A hoe's first time prostituting.
28. **Uncooked** – A hoe that's been hoeing but is not burnt out.

Stacks...

pimpin' for life

OG STACK$

www.ingramcontent.com/pod-product-compliance
Lightning Source LLC
LaVergne TN
LVHW051604070426
835507LV00021B/2762